BEFORE AND BEYOND THE
NIIHAU ZERO

THE UNLIKELY DRAMA OF HAWAII'S FORBIDDEN ISLAND
PRIOR TO, DURING, AND AFTER THE PEARL HARBOR ATTACK

SYD JONES

Before and Beyond the Niihau Zero

Published by:
Signum Ops, 435 Nora Ave., Merritt Island, Florida 32952.

ISBN 978-1500590178
Library of Congress Catalog-in-Publication data:
Jones, Syd
Before and Beyond the Niihau Zero

Graphics by:
Neal Sands

Photos by:
Syd Jones or KT Budde-Jones unless noted otherwise.

This book is dedicated to my life partner, KT Budde-Jones, and our "avian daughter" Ploppy, who spent her last year on my shoulder watching me compile this book.

Contents

Acknowledgements

As with many things in life, this book has contributions from of a broad spectrum of people. I would like to thank Akira Hirayama for his precise interpretation skills, and for acting as an unfailing conduit to WWII Japanese Naval aviators and their experiences. Thanks as well to Arnold and Naomi Kanehiro, who shared personal insights and publications about the fascinating Japanese-American experience in Hawaii. Historians David Aikens and Daniel Martinez both gave numerous valuable perspectives.

Most of the supporting documents found within were located by KT Budde-Jones directly through her own research or through contacts she made. Keith and Bruce Robinson allowed not only access to Niihau Island, the Zero wreckage, Cletrac, and plows, but most importantly, to the Niihau people as well. Keith freely shared his family's history as well as countless invaluable details about the places and people on Niihau where this unique story was staged.

Finally, Mahalo Nui Loa to the many volunteers of the Pacific Aviation Museum, who helped make the dream come true.

Forewords

In the history of the Pearl Harbor attack there are myriad of stories of misfortune, valor, horror, honor and controversy. There is no doubt that all these elements are intertwined in the drama that evolved on the small island of Ni'ihau. The occupation that was perpetrated by a Japanese pilot that crashed landed there went on for five days... from December 7th thru 13th of 1941. This extraordinary episode of history took place on a remote island over a hundred miles west of the battlefield on Oahu. Even today the story is still shrouded by the shadows of mystery, intrigue and the specter of the politics of memory.

During the war scattered reports could be found in the newspapers in New York, Washington and Honolulu. Sketches of what had happened but nothing in definitive nature. The first popular book to shed light on the incident at Ni'ihau was Walter Lord's, *Day of Infamy* in 1957. As a boy I read this account and wondered... how could this have happened and why? What drove men to such a point that an incident among local islanders and a Japanese pilot could end so tragically?

In the early afternoon of that "Day of Infamy", a pilot named Shigenori Nishikaichi arrived at the island with an aircraft crippled by ground fire over Oahu. Returning to his aircraft carrier, the *Hiryu*, was now out of the question. He had chosen the rescue point where a Japanese submarine would be waiting. Moments later he crash landed on the red dirt fields of Niihau. It was as if he fell from the sky into a place as foreign to him as the moon. The remoteness that befell Nishikaichi was also shared by a handful of island workers. The hundred or more Ni'ihauans were secluded and immersed in a plantation system that was reminiscent of an era known to the United States a century before. Outside communication was accomplished through the use of signal fires and supply boats. No radio and no phones existed... isolation.

What transpired over the next five days would add to the legend of the "Forbidden Island". Theft, assault, arson, murder and suicide would be the ingredients for a controversy that still lingers to this day. We may never know how or why the Japanese–American Yoshio Harada sided and abetted with the Japanese aviator. What drove Harada to participate in criminal acts against his neighbors? One can only consider the dynamic of fear and panic that may have driven the pilot Nishikaichi and beekeeper Harada to make such serious transgressions that would ultimately culminate in their deaths. Certainly the actions of one American of Japanese ancestry should not condemn the loyalty of thousands of others. But fear and race would ultimately lead the United

States government to the massive removal of Japanese-Americans from the West Coast to desolate and desperate rural relocation centers.

In the chapters that follow, the author, Syd Jones, carefully navigates you through this fascinating and controversial history. Mr. Jones and his wife KT are aviation experts and aviators of some note and accomplishment. In preparing this manuscript, the author spent years conducting research and discovering new primary source evidence that came in the form of official documents, photography and archeology. He made visits to Ni'ihau documenting the site location of the crash and the village where most of the "Ni'ihau Incident" played out. During that time he gained the confidence and friendship of Mr. Keith Robinson, a direct descendent of the family that has managed the island since the 1860s. On behalf of the Pacific Aviation Museum, Mr. Jones undertook negotiations to acquire wreckage related to the Nishikaichi A6M2 Zero fighter and the Cletrac tractor. Later, those artifacts loaned to the museum from the Robinson family. Currently the aircraft remnants and the tractor are on display at the Pacific Aviation Museum at Pearl Harbor.

The incident at Ni'ihau will probably not be remembered as it was during the war. Folklore and legends were part of the local memory. The saying in the islands that "you have to shoot a Hawaiian three times before he is mad," stems from the shooting of Ben Kanahele by the pilot Nishikaichi. In 1943, a popular song blared on the radio from New York to Honolulu. Titled *"They Couldn't Take Ni'ihau No-how"*, told of the heroism of the Hawaiian Ben Kanahele. Perhaps, that is part of the story that is often eclipsed in other author's renditions.

The painful journey of understanding the critical episodes that unfolded on the island of Ni'ihau in December of 1941, have been carefully crafted by Syd Jones. The attention to detail and the presentation of the facts as he understands them today, knit a contextual historical tapestry that far out shines any scholarship that has been done on this subject thus far.

As a historian, I'm often intrigued by the lessons of history and the incident at Ni'ihau is no exception. Perhaps, the famed Pearl Harbor Historian, Dr. Gordon Prange, said it best with his seminal work, *"At Dawn We Slept"*...

"Pearl Harbor demonstrated one enduring lesson: The unexpected can happen and often does."

Daniel A. Martinez
Pacific War Historian
Pearl Harbor, Hawaii

For World War II history lovers, aviation enthusiasts, and fans of Hawaii, "*Before and Beyond the Niihau Zero*" is a wonderful book to savor.

President Roosevelt said December 7, 1941 was a "day that will live in infamy." Almost every American alive on that day had etched in their memory where they were when they heard the shocking news of Japan's attack on Pearl Harbor. This book tells the story of a small group of Americans who lived very close to Pearl Harbor, but had no knowledge of the raid.

Imagine the chaos when a Japanese pilot landed his Zero on their remote island of Niihau, Hawaii. What happens next is a fascinating story and the author tells it with great detail and sensitivity.

The author has done amazing research no one else has done because of his access to the island and its population. He also uncovered the results of Brigadier General William "Billy" Mitchell's prediction in the 1920s that Japan and the United States would be engaged in a future conflict and the Japanese would use the remote island of Niihau as a staging area for their aircraft. Mitchell was dismissed as a crackpot by the military command.

It is a great read. In todays's world of instantaneous communication, it is almost impossible to believe people residing in the very state that was attacked did not know about it. Yet, what transpired and how they reacted is a very compelling human interest story, and a piece of WWII history few people know.

Pat Schroeder
US Congresswoman 1973-1997
Colorado, District 1

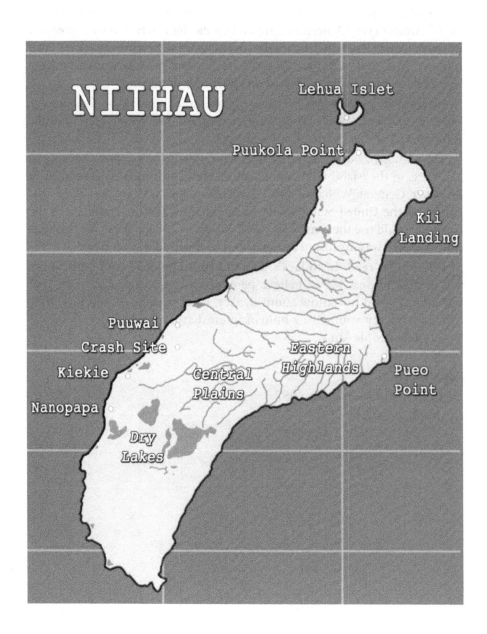

NIIHAU

Lehua Islet

Puukola Point

Kii Landing

Puuwai Crash Site

Kiekie

Nanopapa

Central Plains

Dry Lakes

Eastern Highlands

Pueo Point

PART I

DECEMBER 7, 1941 9:16 am

An overwhelming smell of gasoline compelled Naval Airman 1st Class Shigenori Nishikaichi to break away from his flight. They had just finished fifteen minutes of low-level strafing attacks on the small American air base at Bellows Field on eastern Oahu. He pulled back hard on the control stick, eager to distance himself from further ground fire until he could determine the source of the smell.

The throttle on his A6M2 Zero fighter was still nearly at maximum power as he climbed for safety towards a narrow gap between the scattered clouds above. As the Zero streaked upward, he continued to scan the skies for airborne American fighters but saw none. Nishikaichi was able to look north over a nearby mountain ridge and saw wind clotted black smoke still trailing from fires at distant Kaneohe Naval Air Station. Seconds later, his Zero was up amongst the clouds.

Feeling safe for the moment, Nishikaichi leveled off and pulled the throttle and propeller RPM back on his Zero's engine, its angry exhaust note receding to a rolling baritone. He cracked open the canopy to vent off the fumes welling up in the cockpit. The airplane settled into a cruise, giving the pilot a chance to take stock of his situation.

Despite his adrenaline-boosted concentration during the high-speed strafing attacks on Bellows, Nishikaichi had sensed the Zero taking hits. The impact of the bullets had transmitted directly through the Zero's metal structure into the control stick, rudder bar and even his seat. Right now the engine's sound and its gauges appeared normal and the flight controls still operated smoothly.

Nishikaichi anxiously scanned the surface of his wings through his Plexiglas canopy, spotting something that made his heart sink. A faint white mist trailed from a small hole in the top of the right wing near the fuselage. The aluminum fuel tank mounted just under the wing skin had been punctured, possibly by a bullet having gone completely through the wing. Was the fuselage fuel tank mounted just ahead of his feet or the exterior drop-tank holed as well? The fuel gauges mounted near his left leg didn't immediately confirm his fears. He opened the canopy a little wider, alarmed that the fumes might catch fire.

Nishikaichi's Zero hadn't been hit by airplane-killing, explosive anti-aircraft shells, or the shredding effect of a heavy machine gun. Random small arms ground fire had simply poked a few holes in the aircraft from below, much like a large ice pick. Unfortunately, those holes seemed to be in critical areas.

This was bad. The low pressure on the top of the wing's surface that allowed the Zero to fly was now sucking fuel out of the wing tank through the bullet hole. This was the fuel he needed to get back to his carrier *Hiryu*, far to the north. From take off, Nishikaichi had run his engine off the fuel in his exterior, center-line drop-tank before switching to his fuselage tank just prior to at-

Shigenori Nishikaichi during flight training.
Photo: National Archives

tacking Bellows The long flight south from the fleet to Oahu and the high power used during his attack on Bellows had consumed almost a third of his Zero's gasoline. It was standard procedure to jettison

Distant Niihau Island seen from the western shore of Kauai.

the drop-tank upon meeting enemy fighters, but Nishikaichi hadn't encountered any in the air. Whatever fuel supply remained in the drop-tank as well as the wing and fuselage tanks would determine his fate. His Zero, despite being the most advanced naval fighter in the world, appeared to be bleeding out. His mouth suddenly felt very dry as he realized that he might not be able to rejoin his flight for their return to the carrier.

Nishikaichi was determined not to allow his valuable aircraft or himself to be captured here. He and the other pilots had been instructed that if they couldn't return to their carriers due to battle damage or mechanical problems, to divert to a small, remote island just west of Kauai. A Japanese submarine had been posted there to pick up any aviators that had to land on the island.

The aviator's eventual course would take him to Niihau Island. He did not know his arrival had been anticipated many years before, and that events triggered by his actions there would still remain controversial decades later.

NOW AND THEN

Niihau (pronounced knee-e-how) is rarely acknowledged on tourist maps of the Hawaiian Islands. It's often depicted as an anonymous green blob just to the left of Kauai. There are no tourist resorts

Central Niihau.

or destinations on the island; it is privately owned. Since access by outsiders is tightly controlled and extremely rare, Niihau has gained the nickname "The Forbidden Island."

The unknown nature of the place invites much speculation amongst both tourists and Hawaiian locals alike. Most of these assumptions are incorrect. Niihau simply doesn't fit easily into a box.

Seen at a distance from western Kauai, Niihau's dark, indistinct shape looks mountainous. In truth, Niihau is low and mostly flat — the ridge line running along its eastern shore forms a false front, much like that on an old-west general store.

Tourists sometimes hear stories that Niihau is populated solely by cloistered native Hawaiians, practicing their traditional language, culture and way of life. That usually brings to mind visions from the movie "Mutiny on the Bounty", complete with exotic topless Polynesian maidens and mysterious tiki gods on a pristine, waterfall laced paradise island. Cynical locals speak of the island being a holdover from the bad old days of Hawaiian plantation life, where strict landowners maintained complete feudal control over their overworked, uneducated, and underpaid workforce.

Niihau lacks many of the paradise credentials that other Hawaiian islands enjoy. Neighboring Kauai is touted as the rainiest place on earth, blessed with dramatic waterfalls and an emerald cloak of tropical vegetation. Kauai's high central mountains squeegee all the trade wind moisture out of the air, leaving nothing for downwind Niihau. Even if the winds shift, Niihau's lack of elevation rarely inspires clouds to drop their moisture there. For the most part Niihau is painfully dry, and what water comes out of the ground is brackish.

Niihau unintentionally became a privately owned island as a result of one family's globe spanning odyssey. Captain Francis Sinclair (ex-Royal Navy), his wife Elizabeth, and their family sailed from Scotland to New Zealand in 1839 to raise livestock. Unfortunately, Elizabeth became a widow there in 1846 when her husband was lost at sea. During the ensuing Maori wars in New Zealand, the family found itself in an uncomfortable position, having strong ties on both sides of the conflict.

The decision was made to sell their property in New Zealand and move elsewhere. In the spring of 1863, Elizabeth and her family loaded possessions, cattle and personal wealth in the form of gold aboard their ship *Bessie* and sailed to Canada, looking for an island to buy to establish a ranch. They stopped briefly in Hawaii and Tahiti, to scout possibilities, and then continued onward to Canada. After landfall on Vancouver Island, they decided that the climate in Canada was too cold and wet for ranching. *Bessie's* next stop was a return to Hawaii. They arrived on Oahu in September 1863 hoping to find a suitable ranch location there.

The king of Hawaii at that time, Kamehameha IV, offered them their choice of four sites on Oahu, including what would eventually be known as Ford Island and a tract of land starting about a half mile east of the current Iolani Palace stretching all the way to Diamond Head. Although this last area is now known as Honolulu and Waikiki Beach, the Sinclairs did not find any of the Oahu choices suitable for ranching. He then offered them most of the island of Niihau for $10,000 in gold. By coincidence, Niihau was in a rare rainy cycle, the dry lakes were full of water and the island was verdant in freshly grown grasses. The Sinclairs quickly agreed to the deal.

The king unexpectedly died before the sale went through, and his

Sinclair /Robinson family circa 1889 in Hawaii. Aylmer Robinson is the baby.
Photo: Robinson Collection

successor, Kamehameha V, concluded the deal, after which he made a statement that can be recited by family descendants to this day. "Niihau is now yours, the people that live there will work for you and serve you, but the time may come when the Hawaiian people are not as strong in these islands as they are now. If that day comes, please do what you can to help them." This was accepted as a "gentlemen's agreement" in the eyes of the Scottish Calvinist Sinclairs, an understanding carried on through subsequent generations of the family. The agreement fostered their willingness to accept the continuation of the Hawaiian language and many of the original customs on Niihau. Unintentionally, this would result in the only privately funded aboriginal reserve in existence in Hawaii.

In time the family bought the two smaller remaining tracts of property on Niihau from other private owners, giving them the entire island. While many of Niihau's native population chose to move to Kauai's Na Pali coastline after the Sinclairs took possession of the island, those that wanted to stay were allowed to, many of which found employment on the ranch.

Aylmer Robinson at (approximately) age 73.   Photo: Robinson Collection

Six years later Elizabeth Sinclair expanded her family's land holdings by buying acreage at Makaweli, Kauai. One of Elizabeth's daughters, Helen, had married New Zealander Charles Robinson before the family left New Zealand. Though their pairing was brief, they produced a son named Aubrey. Aubrey Robinson grew up in Hawaii and eventually attended law school in Boston. He married Alice Gay, producing five children. Aubrey's relationship with the Gays broadened when he started a sugar plantation partnership on Kauai with Francis Gay. Of critical importance to this story was Aubrey's second son, Aylmer.

Aylmer Robinson would ascend within the family business after receiving a degree from Harvard University, where he graduated near the very top of his class. Aylmer followed the family tradition, working for a time outside the family business before assuming the position of business manager of the Gay and Robinson plantation. Sometime around 1922 he took over the management of the Niihau ranch.

Like earlier members of his family, Aylmer was fluent in the Hawaiian language. This was a practical rather than an academic skill - it was simply the easiest way to communicate with the Niihau people, even though by now they all had at least a basic understanding of English. The church that missionaries had built on Niihau before the island was purchased was still in use, and the Sinclair/Robinsons additionally maintained a school there.

Aylmer had taken on a serious challenge in trying to keep the ranch solvent. He was determined to employ as many of the Niihau people as he could, but after 1932 numerous personal cash infusions were required to make payroll. If an extended drought hit the already dry island, the stock could all easily be wiped out. Because of Niihau's remoteness, Aylmer spent part of his time directing operations on Niihau and the rest tending the ranch's business affairs from Makaweli, Kauai. An outbreak of measles had gone through the island's indigenous population, killing eleven children and scarring others for life. From that point, Aylmer denied outsider access to Niihau without his permission to minimize any further exposure of the islanders to disease. As Aylmer labored to sustain his backwater ranch, an outspoken American Army officer thousands of miles away was also considering Niihau. His view of the island's future was much different than any of the Robinsons [1].

It seemed that Brigadier General William "Billy" Mitchell had managed to confront, embarrass or enrage just about all of the "old school" admirals and generals in the U.S. military. Mitchell was the first American officer to fly over enemy lines in WWI and had subsequently led the largest number of bombers to fly on a single

---

1   Robinson/author interviews 12/05, 1/06, 5/06, 8/12

Brigadier General Billy Mitchell   Photo: National Archives

mission during the conflict — fifteen hundred planes. Mitchell's experiences during the war only reinforced his view that aviation would eventually render traditional weapons and military strategy obsolete. He was eager to promote his vision and was dismissive of traditional military thinking.

Billy Mitchell has been described as an airpower evangelist, envisioning a future where aircraft became the dominant military asset. He was quite public in pitching his opinions that both battleships and traditional land armies were now obsolete, that in the future massed airpower could sink any warship or fly over any army to destroy an enemy's cities, factories and military installations.

Mitchell staged demonstrations of his ideas by sinking captured or obsolete battleships with airplanes. He advocated an independent air force, and was relentlessly and publicly critical of both the Navy and Army perspective that aviation was subservient to their traditional roles. Billy's opinions weren't expressed only through military channels; he also stirred the pot by speaking openly to the press.

General Mason Patrick decided that it was important to silence Mitchell — at least for a while. A mission inspecting foreign air power in the Pacific and Asia was invented to keep Billy occupied and away from the press. Mitchell took the assignment seriously, departing for nine months with his new wife shortly after their wedding in the fall of 1923. Hawaii, Midway, Guam, the Philippines, and particularly Japan were all on his agenda along with mainland Asian countries. He watched military maneuvers, analyzed offensive and defensive potentials, considered military preparedness and observed nationalistic trends. During the trip back, Mitchell began putting the sum of his experience and opinions into written form.

In Mitchell's theories of the future, Japan and America would be opponents in an upcoming war. He envisioned this new conflict starting with a Japanese sneak attack against American naval, ground, and air forces on the Hawaiian island of Oahu, beginning at Pearl Harbor's Ford Island. In his prediction, the attack would occur early on a Sunday morning (7:30 am), simultaneous with a Japanese invasion of the Philippines. The Japanese would also move against English and European colonies in the Pacific.

Mitchell felt that the Japanese would start their campaign against Hawaii by first establishing a base on Midway and then transporting aircraft to Niihau Island. In his own words; "As soon as set up and tested, those ships (aircraft) would fly to Niihau and be ready to attack Oahu immediately." Niihau would serve as a forward air base, allowing continued attacks on Oahu military installations as well as Honolulu [2].

Billy Mitchell presented his report in a 323 page document titled

---

2   Billy Mitchell, James J. Cooke, The Billy Mitchell Affair, Burke Davis page 174
      Random House

"Report on inspection of U.S. possessions in the Pacific and Java, Singapore, India, Siam, China and Japan" to General Patrick in October 1924. Many of Mitchell's critics immediately set about to discredit or belittle his opinions and predictions.

Mitchell's bold statements and criticisms had created many enemies in the military, but he also had some loyal and prominent disciples. One was Major Gerald C. Brant, a true believer in the Mitchell doctrine and one of the first to read his Pacific report. When Mitchell's overt accusations of incompetence towards the Navy and War department finally triggered his own court-martial in October 1925, Brant testified on Billy Mitchell's behalf, joined by America's leading WWI ace Eddie Rickenbacker, and future Army Air Force superstars Major Carl Spaatz and Major "Hap" Arnold.

During the trial, the assistant prosecutor praised Brant's honesty, but then derided Brant and the others testifying for Mitchell. He stated that they had been infected by Mitchell's "grandiose schemes." The trial did not end in Billy Mitchell's favor, and shortly thereafter he resigned his commission. Mitchell may have lost an important fo-

Major Gerald Brant   Photo: National Archives

rum to influence military aviation, but the power of his ideas lived on in officers like Brant.

In the spring of 1931, Gerald Brant was posted as an Air Officer in the Hawaiian Department. He had risen to the rank of Lt. Colonel, and was the Commanding Officer of the 18ᵗʰ Composite Wing based at Ft. Shafter on Oahu. It was the same year that Japan invaded Manchuria. As a military man, Brant was no doubt aware of Japan's distant belligerence. Would war eventually come to Hawaii as Billy Mitchell had prophesied? Brant knew he was stationed at the epicenter of Billy's prediction. It was the perfect opportunity for him to pursue his belief in the soundness of Mitchell's ideas.

Billy Mitchell's hunch that the remote Niihau Island might be used as a forward air base for aerial attacks on Oahu had been well considered:

1. Unlike the other Hawaiian Islands, there was an abundance of flat land — a perfect location to quickly establish air operations.
2. The high but narrow ridge along the eastern shore of the island would hide inland activities from neighboring Kauai.
3. There was no direct communication between Niihau and any of the other Hawaiian Islands.
4. Travel to or from the island was limited to the occasional enterprising Niihau resident transporting pigs to Kauai's isolated Na Pali coast by outrigger canoe or the regular trips from Makaweli by Aylmer Robinson aboard his family owned "sampan" workboat.
5. There were few inhabitants and no military presence on the island.
6. It was less than one hour's flight time to Oahu, and of Hawaii's eight main islands was the closest to Japan.

The Robinson family's substantial land holdings along with their agricultural and livestock business made them a large presence in Hawaii, particularly on Kauai. It didn't prove too difficult for Lt. Colonel Brant to identify the owners of Niihau and make arrangements to meet with Aylmer Robinson at Makaweli.

According to Robinson family history, the meeting occurred secretly in 1933. This was the same year that Japan withdrew from the

The primary transportation to and from Niihau was aboard the Robinson sampan "Lehua".   Photo: Robinson Collection

League of Nations over criticism of its activities in China, where it had recently captured an inner Mongolian province. News of Japan's increasingly warlike activities against China made newspapers all over the world, and in mid-Pacific Hawaii the trouble felt uncomfortably close.

The exact content of Lt. Colonel Brant's discussion with Aylmer was not recorded, but the results proved that Brant had been convincing. During the course of their talk, Brant showed Aylmer the portion of Mitchell's report that stated Niihau's possible role. The Robinson's family history also holds that Aylmer and an Army officer, possibly Brant, were later seen examining Niihau from horseback. Brant and Aylmer worked out a solution for Mitchell's presumption that Niihau would be used as a staging area for Japanese aerial attacks on Oahu. Since this was an "unofficial" project based largely on Mitchell's prediction, there would be no government involvement or money to assist. It would fall solely on Aylmer's shoulders to ensure its completion, at his own expense and in absolute secrecy.

Aylmer Robinson was a man of the same moral convictions as his Sinclair ancestors. Like them, a handshake agreement was a contract, and Aylmer had committed to Brant's plan. In order to keep Niihau from being used as an airfield by the Japanese, the island would be crosshatched with deeply plowed furrows. The furrows were to be laid out in squares like a giant checkerboard. Each square would be about one hundred feet across, the furrows about two and a half feet wide and twenty inches deep. To make doubly sure that an aircraft couldn't land, in some places a second parallel furrow was placed immediately adjacent to others in a square. Any aircraft attempting to land amongst the furrows would have its landing gear torn off and/or be flipped on its back.

The project started not long after the meeting between Brant and Aylmer. The plowing was started using heavy draft animals, a hot and

Most furrows today are eroded or overgrown, but some are visible on Niihau's drylakes.

thirsty job in Niihau's arid climate. The plan was for the furrows to cover every part of the island where an airplane could land. It was a huge and slowly realized endeavor.

Lt. Col. Brant would not be on hand to see the project completed. He was transferred to his next posting on the mainland in 1934. Mitchell's prophecy was now in Aylmer's hands.

In February 1936 Billy Mitchell died, never seeing the future events he had envisioned. Brant had been promoted to full Colonel and was currently the commanding officer of the 3rd Wing, General Headquarters Air Force in Louisiana. Aylmer continued overseeing the slowly advancing plowing of his tiny island far out in the Pacific.

Japan's expansionism rose to an alarming level the following year. After several years of small but increasing "incidents" against China, Japan launched into total war. The "Rape of Nanking" was a result of this new level of violence. Japan's accelerating offensive in China spilled over, this time involving Americans.

The *USS Panay* was a large U.S. Navy river gunboat that was sent up the Yangtze River to evacuate U.S. embassy staff and European nationals from the city of Nanking as Japanese forces moved to overrun the city. Because the U.S. was a neutral country, steaming into a war zone was a risky mission. *Panay* was clearly marked with oversize U.S. flags hung on her upper decks and flagstaff [3].

After retrieving the Americans and Europeans, *Panay* departed Nanking. Flights of Japanese aircraft attacked and sank *Panay* as it lay anchored south of the city. The crew put up a valiant defense, but several U.S. sailors were killed and nearly half of the crew and passengers were wounded. By chance, a couple of reporters with film cameras were on board and filmed the attack. When the news and films reached America, it caused a national outrage. The Japanese government quickly made official apologies, claiming that the attack was accidental since the high altitude bombers couldn't see the displayed American flags, however the films taken during the incident clearly showed low flying Japanese warplanes repeatedly strafing the well-marked gunboat.

---

3   *USS Panay* memorial website

To Aylmer Robinson this was a frightening escalation. It seemed to be a prelude to the events that Brant and he had discussed. The horse-drawn plowing of Niihau was continuing, but very slowly. Aylmer decided he needed to step up the pace of the project since the Japanese had now boldly attacked American interests. He ordered and paid for a small, multi-purpose tractor called a "Cletrac" from the Cleveland Tractor Company on the mainland. The Cletrac was about the size of a Jeep but looked like a mini-bulldozer, having tracks instead of wheels. It would be the perfect implement to accelerate the plowing of Niihau's hard soil.

The plowing operation shifted into high gear when the Cletrac arrived, but much of the island had yet to be worked. Unlike a horse, the Cletrac didn't require food, water, or rest, but deep furrowing the volcanic soil was still slow. Joseph Keoua Kele drove the machine while Oliva Kamala, Kauileilehua Keamoai and Kamakaukiuli Kawahalau cleared brush and rolled away boulders in front of it. As the Cletrac drawn plow advanced across Niihau's red dirt, the Japanese too advanced their war footing in Asia. From Niihau, it almost seemed like a race to destiny.

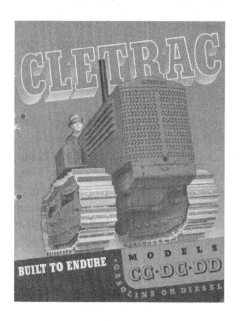

A 1937 Cletrac brochure (the model pictured is larger than the one used on Niihau).

The plowing of Niihau was finally completed in the summer of 1941. Thousands of linear miles of furrows were in place. Other than steep slopes, the settlement of Puuwai, and exceptionally rocky areas, any land deemed suitable for aircraft operations was ruined for that purpose. It had been an extraordinary enterprise; for over seven years a private citizen had prepared and funded a bulwark against a theoretical Japanese attack of unknown likelihood. It also changed the character of the place. Movement by vehicle any distance on Niihau now required traversing the endless furrows. It was an unpleasant addition to life on the island.

Aylmer had fulfilled his obligation in the agreement with Brant, and if Japan's Chinese/western Pacific war moved towards Hawaii, his furrows were ready. All he could do now was refocus on the business of Niihau ranch, follow the news, and wait.

In the meantime, Japan had dramatically expanded its conquest of China and mounted the invasion of Indochina. Britain and the U.S. both froze Japanese assets, in addition, the U.S. embargoed the sale of raw materials and oil to Japan. By the time the U.S. Navy had been put on alert at end of November 1941, the Japanese had finished their plans for a surprise aerial attack on America's naval forces at Pearl Harbor, as well as other military installations on Oahu, Hawaii. There would be attacks on Guam, Wake Island, and the Philippines as well. Billy Mitchell had predicted in 1924 that the surprise air raid would occur at 7:30 am on a Sunday morning, initially targeting Pearl Harbor's Ford Island. The actual Japanese attack was on Sunday, December 7, 1941 with the first bombs landing on Ford Island just before 8:00 am.

Mitchell's remarkable prophecy wasn't completely accurate. The

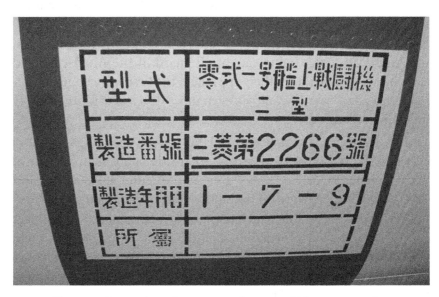

The manufacturer's production stencil as it would have appeared on Nishikaichi's Zero.

Japanese didn't plan to launch the attack from Niihau as he had stated. Instead, the Japanese planes took off from six aircraft carriers supported by a vast task force to the north of Oahu. The "Forbidden Island" would serve a different role in the Japanese plans.

About the same time that the plowing was finished on Niihau, the construction of a Mitsubishi A6M2 model 21 Zero fighter, manufacture number 2266, was completed at its factory in Japan. The fate of this aircraft, its pilot and Niihau Island would become inseparable from the actual day of the Japanese attack onward through history.

BELLOWS

The aerial component of the December 7, 1941 Japanese raid on Hawaii began with a dangerous pre-dawn, rough seas launching of the first wave attack force. One hundred and eighty nine aircraft took off from the pitching decks of their six carriers in the dark, beginning at about 6:00 am (local time) while the task force was still approximately 230 nautical miles north of Oahu. In fifteen minutes the aircraft had formed up and were heading southbound towards Oahu. The success of their attack was largely dependent on the American forces being caught off guard. If the Americans had somehow gotten wind of their approach, the first wave could be flying into a buzz–saw. It would be even more disastrous for the closely following second wave.

The first wave's formation to Oahu was in groupings; torpedo carrying "Kate" bombers were on the left side flying at an altitude of 9,200 feet, bomb loaded "Kates" were in the center at 9,800 feet, and "Val" dive bombers were on the right at just over 11,000 feet. "Zero" fighters covered the attack airplanes to the rear at about 14,000 feet [4]. The second wave's formation would be similar, except that there would no torpedo carrying bombers. Japanese planners anticipated that the Americans would quickly recover, and the low-and-slow torpedo bombers would be easy targets

---

4   Pearl Harbor, H.P. Willmott, Cassel &Co.

Shortly after 7:00 am the Japanese fleet turned once more into the wind, building speed to prepare for the launch of the second wave. Shigenori Nishikaichi ran with the other pilots and aircrew to their assigned planes staged on the aircraft carrier *Hiryu's* deck.

The aircraft had already been started and warmed up by maintenance personnel. The engine's vibrations, and wings caught in the gusty breeze over the flight deck caused the planes to shiver like anxious racehorses. Early morning sunlight flickered against the propeller arcs, and the noise of so many unmuffled engines only added to the tense excitement of the moment. When Nishikaichi arrived at his Zero fighter, it was hard to hear any irregularities in its engine's sound with so much similar noise all around him. He traded places in the cockpit with a maintenance crewman, who helped him strap in. Nishikaichi did a final check of the airplane's controls and instruments, and then made sure that his navigational maps and briefing notes were at hand.

Shigenori Nishikaichi's A6M2 Zero had maneuverability and range that far exceeded any fighters in the American Navy at the time of the Pearl Harbor attack. The Zeros were armed with both machine guns and cannons, and until Allied pilots developed tactics to deal with the lithe fighter, they usually died fighting it. The Zero had a small engine compared to American designs, but its lightly

A restored A6M2 Zero painted in the same markings as Shigenori Nishikaichi's.

built airframe gave decent speed, superb aerobatic capability and the ability to fly long distances on minimal fuel. The Zero was almost mythical to America and its Allies early in the war.

Countless hours of training had led to this moment; Nishikaichi and his fellow pilots were ready, professional and eager to demonstrate the Empire's might against America. The only unknown was the level of American preparedness. The Japanese fleet still had no word about the fate of the first wave.

At 7:15 am the second wave aircraft began launching off all six aircraft carriers. "Kate" bombers took off from *Zuikaku* and *Shokaku* (5th Carrier Division). *Kaga* and *Akagi* (1st Carrier Division) sent aloft "Val" dive-bombers and "Zero" fighters. Additional flights of "Vals" and "Zeros" were dispatched from *Soryu* and *Hiryu* (2nd Carrier Division).

Nishikaichi's plane was one of nine Zero fighters that *Hiryu* launched for the second wave. One of them immediately had engine problems and quickly returned to *Hiryu*. As on the first wave, the Zeros climbed to an altitude above the rest of the attack aircraft, following the massed formation towards Oahu. The *Hiryu* planes all had two vertical blue stripes around the rear fuselage and "BII" for identification preceding the tail number. *Soryu's* aircraft had one vertical blue stripe, *Akagi's* had one red stripe, *Kaga's* had two red stripes, *Shokaku's* had one white stripe and *Zuikaku's* planes had two white stripes.

The plan was to fly south directly towards Oahu. At a predetermined point just north of the island the second wave aerial armada of 167 aircraft would merge into defensive formations that would then depart towards their respective assigned targets. As hoped, the first wave's attack had caught the Americans off guard, and had already inflicted serious damage. The second wave would be the final of a deadly one-two punch against the bloodied U.S. forces. Ironically, the Americans had themselves squandered warnings of the oncoming attack; information about the early morning sinking of a Japanese mini-submarine trying to enter Pearl Harbor and a radar report of a large formation of aircraft (the Japanese first wave) approaching Oahu was bungled instead of sounding the alarm.

The *Hiryu* Zeros' orders were to continue south to Oahu, then follow near the eastern shore towards Kaneohe Naval Air Station. Kaneohe was an important target for both waves, largely due to the long-range PBY patrol seaplanes that were based there. These seaplanes had the range, capability and potential to locate the Japanese fleet and direct an American counterstrike. On this heading, the *Hiryu* Zeros could join the second wave attack by strafing Kaneohe before continuing on to Bellows Field, further to the south. If their ammunition supply allowed it, they could hit Kaneohe again on their way back to the fleet. Above all, the Zero fighters were to intercept any airborne American planes that might challenge the Japanese attack aircraft.

The Japanese planners had not valued Bellows Field as highly as other Oahu targets for the raid. Pearl Harbor Naval Air Station (Ford Island), Pearl Harbor, Hickam and Wheeler Army Air Fields, Ewa Marine Corps Air Field and Kaneohe Naval Air Station all suffered concentrated attacks from both waves. The first wave attack on Bellows was comprised of a single Zero making one brief strafing pass.

Originally Bellows had been a satellite installation for Wheeler Army Air Field, but during the summer of 1941 had emerged as a separate military post. Bellows was remote, and living conditions for the personnel based there were rudimentary compared to the more developed Hickam or Wheeler facilities. It had only one tarmac runway whose departure end faced the open ocean and one of the nicest beaches on Oahu. The only permanent aircraft based there were a few small observation types of the 86th Observation Squadron. The field was currently being used by fighter squadrons practicing aerial gunnery. In early November 1941, the 44th Pursuit Squadron from Wheeler Field deployed to Bellows with its twelve P-40B fighters, pilots and ground crews for a month long exercise. A B-18 bomber detailed from Hickam Field to tow aerial targets for the fighters was also on hand.

On Saturday, December 6, 1941, the fighters flew more scheduled gunnery training. When they finished that afternoon, they were parked empty of fuel and ammunition. Normal practice at Bellows was for the aircraft to be serviced and have the guns cleaned on Sunday for the following week's missions. All but three of the 44th Squadron's pilots left Bellows for the remainder of the weekend. The weapons allocated for the ground defense of Bellows (including .30 and .50 caliber machine guns and 20mm artillery) were locked in the Armory by order [5].

The Sunday morning post-dawn calm at Bellows didn't last long on December 7. News spread quickly through the men in the Bellows tents of frantic communications from both Kaneohe and Hickam, both already having suffered the stunning, hammer-fist blows from the Japanese first wave. A lone Zero then approached Bellows Field from over the ocean and made a single strafing pass along the tent area before disappearing to the north. The Bellows men quickly drew weapons from the Armory, but lack of ammunition limited them to Springfield rifles, Browning Automatic Rifles and three .30 caliber machine guns for defense. Ground crewmen hastily began arming and servicing the parked P-40 fighters.

Adding to the confusion of the moment, a smoking Boeing B-17C Flying Fortress appeared over Bellows, attempting to make an emergency landing. The large, four-engined bomber was one of twelve that had just arrived on Oahu after a long ferry flight from the U.S. mainland, unknowingly arriving in the middle of the Japanese attack. The unarmed B-17s were supposed to land at Hickam, but first wave Zeros engaged in attacking that base also set upon them. Lt. Robert Richards was flying the last of the bombers in line to land. His plane was particularly hard hit, and he sped away to the east towards Bellows to escape. The aircraft had sustained extensive damage, had three seriously wounded crew members on board, and was nearly out of fuel.

The short fighter airstrip at Bellows was of insufficient length for the big B-17 to land in the best of conditions. Lt. Richard's desperate final approach flying with the wind instead of against it assured that the bomber would run out of runway. The Flying Fortress touched down mid-field, and after going off the end of the runway, slid to a stop in a neighboring cane field. Fortunately, there was no further

---

5   7 December 1941, the Air Force story L. Arakaki & J. Kuborn, Pacific Air Forces, Office of History, Hickam Airforce Base, Hawaii, 1981

injury to its crew, and ground personnel helped treat the injured and secured the top-secret Norden bombsight from the airplane.

At about 9:00 am the second wave *Hiryu* Zeros arrived from the north to attack Bellows. The Americans on the ground later reported that they saw nine Zeros; three groups of three aircraft each in "V" formations approaching the field [6]. This number was erroneous, there were actually only eight, (two flights of three and one flight of two) but the inaccurate observation can probably be attributed to the "fog of war." Nishikaichi was flying in one of the flights of three.

Lt. Richards' B-17 crash landed at Bellows   Photo: National Archives

The entire formation of Zero fighters descended on the field, strafing once as a group before breaking up into three flights that each continued strafing attacks from different directions. The Bellows defenders fired back at the attackers as best they could, even using a machine gun mounted in the rear cockpit of one of the parked observation planes.

When their planes were finally fueled and armed, the three American pilots at Bellows tried to get airborne to meet the attackers. Nishikaichi and his fellow *Hiryu* Zero pilots were just as deter-

---

6   7 December 1941, The Air Force Story

mined to destroy them where they were. 2nd Lt. Hans Christiansen was killed by one of the strafing Zeros just as he tried to climb into his cockpit. Pilot Officer 1st Class Tusguo Matsuyama led his wingman, Pilot Officer 1st Class Toshio Makinoda (the flight of two Zeros), against the other two P-40s trying to take off. Matsuyama's guns hit 2nd Lt. George Whiteman just as his P-40 became airborne, causing Whiteman to fatally crash on the beach. 2nd Lt. Samuel Bishop managed to take off and stayed low out over the water, trying to gain

A damaged P-40 fighter after the attack on Bellows.   Photo: National Archives

speed. Matsuyama spotted Bishop's P-40 and made a diving attack, wounding the American pilot and forcing him to crash in the ocean. Bishop survived, and swam to shore [7].

The Japanese second wave attack on Bellows lasted about 15 minutes. Surrounded by damaged and destroyed aircraft and equipment, the American defenders felt they had not been able to inflict any real vengeance on the departing Zeros. They did not know that some of their return fire had actually found its mark. Shigenori Nishikaichi's punctured fuel tanks were leaking away his chances to return to *Hiryu*. He had some decisions to make.

---

7   Pearl Harbor's lost P-36, Flight Journal, David Aiken, October 2002

THE CRASH

Nishikaichi's A6M2 Zero had three internal fuel tanks and one external drop-tank. Two wing tanks holding 50.2 gallons each and a 38.3 gallon fuselage tank mounted just ahead of the pilot were built into the airplane. The 87.2 gallon drop-tank was centrally mounted under the fuselage, between the wings. Since the drop-tank was expendable and was usually jettisoned for improved maneuverability and safety when engaging an enemy plane, its fuel was used first. Once the drop-tank's fuel was gone, the pilot would usually select the fuselage tank, using its contents before choosing one of the wing tanks. Nishikaichi likely selected the still full fuselage tank just before the actual attack on Bellows began, to eliminate the possibility of fuel starvation from the dwindling contents of the drop-tank during his dangerous low-level strafing runs.

The second wave had launched approximately 200 nautical miles north of Oahu, and the distance from the northern tip of Oahu to Bellows added about 25 more to the trip. The combined formation's airspeed was about 150 knots-dictated by the pace of the slowest attack aircraft. This speed would have been a slow trot for the escorting Zeros, at this speed Nishikaichi's aircraft would have been consuming an economical 30 gallons of fuel an hour [8]. Factor in a wind direction of 70 degrees at about 35 knots as reported in Japanese records and the second wave had a theoretical ground speed of about 155 knots. (Note: The winds were stronger at the raid's launch position, velocities reported on Oahu were of a more typical 10-20 knot trade wind day.)

What this all means is that without other considerations, a direct course from the carriers to Bellows should have taken Nishikaichi about one hour and twenty six minutes, while burning about 44 gallons of gasoline — about half the contents of his drop-tank. The actual flight reportedly took 14 minutes longer than this simple time/speed/distance model. There are several reasons for this; the real distance from the fleet to Oahu may have been further than the Japanese navigators estimated at launch time, the climb to assigned

---

8   S. Hinton, Planes of Fame, Chino, California, A6M5 operator, interview 2012

altitudes would be at a slower airspeed and extra time was expended during the formation regroup just north of Oahu. Additional fuel burn would be expected for the same reasons. After 15 minutes of high power/high speed strafing runs on Bellows, Nishikaichi's Zero would have consumed enough fuel at that point to have equaled the entire contents of his drop-tank.

With his normal reserves, Nishikaichi would have had more than enough gasoline to make it back to *Hiryu* after leaving Bellows. The distance back to his carrier would actually be less on the return leg of his flight due to the Japanese fleet's continued progress towards Oahu, intentionally closing the distance to give any crippled returning aircraft a better chance. Unfortunately, the actual rate of fuel loss due to ground fire damage may have been difficult for him to determine, perhaps initially seeming more rapid than it really was. The Japanese submarine waiting just offshore of Niihau for pilots of badly damaged aircraft no doubt took on a larger presence in his decision making process.

Once he decided to fly to Niihau, Nishikaichi had to decide on a route. Retracing his flight path back to Oahu's northernmost point would require traveling 25 nautical miles, from there the west–northwest course to Niihau added another 124, a total of almost 150 nautical miles. This track would distance him from any airborne defenders over Oahu's largest air bases, and he would only need 30 gallons of gas to make a one-hour flight at 150 knots. Another option would have been for him to fly straight from Bellows to Niihau; however, this more direct path added more risk to the 140 nautical mile flight. He would have had to burn more fuel to climb over the Koolau Mountains with their associated highly stacked clouds, then traverse the entirety of Oahu, passing very near Wheeler Field and any of its surviving fighters. Either of these scenarios, calculated without winds, would have placed him over Niihau at roughly 10:15 am. Surprisingly, his actual landing there wasn't until around noon.

No one today knows the exact course that Nishsikaichi followed immediately after he departed from Bellows Field. Certainly, the unaccountably long period of time between his departure from

Bellows and his landing on Niihau invites speculation. In his book *"The Niihau Incident"*, author Allan Beekman identified a lone Hiryu Zero that joined up with second wave *Soryu* Zeros flying near Kaneohe as Nishikaichi's. Beekman even gave credit to Nishikaichi for shooting down one of the P-36 fighters from Wheeler Field that intercepted the combined group of Japanese planes. Subsequent detailed research by historian David Aiken rejects this scenario; he states that the lone *Hiryu* Zero that joined the *Soryu* flight was actually flown by Tusguo Matsuyama, who was low on ammunition and had separated from his flight near Bellows after his two victories there. Matsuyama quickly dropped out of the aerial contest between the Zeros and the Wheeler P-36s without shooting down any of them due to his lack of ammunition [9].

Another confusing story is that of two Curtiss Soc-1 Seagull seaplanes from the *USS Northampton* that traded fire with a Japanese Zero north of Kauai. Some authors have claimed that the Zero was Nishikaichi's but interviews and further research by David Aiken point to a different aircraft.

On Niihau island, parishioners standing outside the church saw two airplanes flying low overhead just before noon, one smoking and obviously in distress. Nearby resident Hawila "Howell" (sometimes erroneously referred to as "Howard") Kaleohano later reported;

"I was outside my house, just before lunch time, when I saw these two planes fly over. One looked like it was in trouble and the other one was flying all around it. Then this first plane goes down in the ocean. The other one flies around some more and then goes away…"

In Beekman's version of this sighting, the damaged aircraft was flown by Naval Airman 2nd Class Saburo Ishii from the *Soryu*, accompanied by Nishikaichi. Additional research by Aiken detailing the story of *Soryu* Fighter Second *Shotai* commander, Lieutenant Fusata Fujita, leads to another conclusion. Fujita was flying his damaged Zero from Kaneohe towards the rallying point near Oahu's northwest Kaena Point following two other *Soryu* Zeros flown by Ishii and Pilot Officer 1st Class Takeshi Atsumi. From his trailing position, Fujita watched as Atsumi and Ishii were attacked near

9   Pearl Harbor's lost p-36, Flight Journal, David Aiken

Above: The Niihau church as it appeared in 1941.
Photo: Robinson Collection
Below: The same church today. The two palm trees planted in front dur-
ing the 1970s are extremely rare native Niihau Fan Palms, scientific
name Pritchardia Aylmer-Robinsoni.

Kaena Point by American P-36s flown by Lieutenant Harry Brown and 2nd Lieutenant Malcom Moore from Wheeler Field. Both Brown and Fujita later described "a big fire" coming from Atsumi's aircraft, which was last seen heading west of Kaena Point (towards Niihau). Ishii's Zero was also hit but was not seen to go down. Since neither pilot made it back to the *Soryu,* it's likely that these two may have been the pair of aircraft that Kaleohano and the Niihau church goers spotted overflying the island.

Minutes after the flight of two Zeros were seen flying over Niihau, Nishikaichi's plane thumped down near Howell Kaleohano's house. Nishikaichi had been in the air approximately an additional two hours and forty-five minutes AFTER the Bellows attack. Clearly, with that endurance, he would have had enough fuel to make it back to his carrier if he had departed for *Hiryu* immediately after Bellows. What kept him from returning with the rest of his flight?

Unfortunately, there are no credible sightings of Nishikaichi's Zero during the time between the Bellows attack and his crash landing on Niihau. The movements of all Japanese aircraft involved in the Pearl Harbor Raid have been studied in minute detail by historians and military analysts for years, yet Nishikaichi's exact flight path between the time he left Bellows and his arrival on Niihau remains unclear. For nearly three hours he continued to fly in Hawaiian airspace without any surviving participants noting his presence. The time in which he was missing remains one of the unresolved mysteries of the Pearl Harbor attack.

David Aiken has suggested that a photo taken from Ford Island

Is this Nishikaichi's Zero over Pearl Harbor?   Photo: National Archives

might have captured an image of Nishikaichi's Zero. The photo shows the very top of the Battleship *Nevada's* mast at the bottom of the frame and a Zero in silhouette trailing smoke or vapor. From the location of the photographer and *Nevada*, the Zero would have been heading south when the photo was taken. Aiken's proposal that this image might be of Nishikaichi is based on the process of elimination, but questions about Nishikaichi's possible motives for flying an already damaged airplane into intense, heavy anti-aircraft fire over large targets that he wasn't briefed to hit make this scenario improbable.

There are several possibilities, but perhaps the simplest explanation for Nishikaichi landing on Niihau instead of returning to *Hiryu* was that he initially overestimated the amount of fuel loss his airplane had suffered. By the time he realized his mistake by extending his flight time over Hawaiian waters, he had already burned through the gasoline that could have taken him home. Ironically, as he glided to an uncertain landing on Niihau, much of the second wave attack force had already landed on their carriers. The last of the second wave was recovered by 12:15 p.m. [10]

As Nishikaichi approached Niihau, he was no doubt looking hard for any sign of the Japanese submarine stationed near the south of the island. The I-74 of the Third Submarine Group was skippered by Commander Ikezawa Masayuki, and had been tasked with plane-watch duty off Niihau.[11] Some sources state that the sub had already departed the area by the time Nishikaichi landed, but mysterious lights were reportedly seen offshore by Niihau residents for several nights after his arrival [12].

Aylmer's plowing had ruined any easy landing options on Niihau. The furrows were easily visible from the air. The best option was probably a beach landing, but Nishikaichi's fuel and luck ran out before he could survey the best area.

When the engine finally quit, Nishikaichi was forced to quickly pick a landing spot and set up for a dead-stick, gliding approach.

10   Pearl Harbor's lost Pt-36, Flight Journal, David Aiken
11   Pearl Harbor, H.P. WIllmott, Cassel and Company
12   Robinson interview, 2013

Nishikaichi's final approach was from the lower right corner of the picture. He hoped to land in the area near where the green and pink houses stand today. The fence still runs from the lower left portion of the picture to the red dirt area in the middle of the photo.

The wind was blowing from the east-northeast, so he approached from the opposite direction to have the slowest possible ground speed upon landing. His intended touchdown would be on a small, flat area between a few scattered houses, but during his descent he had to glide over a rising, up-slope gradient to get there. A fence line perpendicular to his path approximately marked the transition from slope to plateau — if he could make it over the fence the landing might not be so bad if he could get the plane down to the slowest possible speed. He could not see any plow furrows near the houses or on the up-slope.

He slid his canopy back fully, checked his seat belts and put down the flaps and landing gear, slowing the Zero to just above stall speed. Putting the landing gear down for an off-field landing like this was risky, if the wheels caught in a depression or hit a solid object like a rock, the airplane could easily be flipped on its back. Another unusual detail was that the drag-inducing external drop-tank was still attached to the bottom the plane between the landing gear. Any unusable fuel left in the low-slung tank was a potential fire hazard if it hit an obstruction during this type of uncertain landing. (Note: Nishikaichi may not have been able to release his drop-tank, corrosion from extended salt air exposure was reported to have affected the ability of other Pearl Harbor Zeros to jettison their external tanks.)

In the gusty wind conditions it was hard to judge the best approach angle. Nishikaichi got the Zero's airspeed so slow that the propeller stopped wind-milling just before the impact. Unfortunately, the upslope terrain was rising fast; in the last seconds of flight it was apparent the plane would hit the ground just short of reaching the fence line. The hill looked like it was covered with soft grasses; Nishiskaichi didn't know that it hadn't been plowed because of the many large rocks hidden amongst the weeds.

The Zero hit very hard on its main gear just before blowing through the wire fence. Simultaneously, both main landing gear struts sheared off at their pivot points. A large rock caught the right wing's landing gear strut as it wrenched away, spinning the airplane about 80 degrees to the right. The empty drop-tank was ripped from its mount as the airplane slid over it, and the stress of torsional loads on the lightly built airframe rippled the fuselage skin behind the cockpit and near the engine mount. The Zero's rate of deceleration was extreme — from initial impact to final resting spot was less than 70 feet.

Within the red cloud of dust thrown up by the crash was a potentially unique and valuable prize to the American military; on U.S. soil was a momentarily stunned, but live Japanese pilot who had participated in the Pearl Harbor raid, and a damaged but repairable A6M2 Zero Fighter. Unfortunately, the authorities knew nothing of it. The Americans would not get another chance to get their hands on an intact Zero conveniently deposited on U.S. territory until six months later, when Flight Petty Officer Tadayoshi Koga attempted to land his battle damaged Zero in a bog in Alaska's Aleutian Islands during the Midway offensive. Like Nishikaichi, Koga chose to extend his landing gear, and his drop-tank was still in place when he touched down. Koga's landing gear and drop-tank also sheared off as his plane's wheels dug in and the airplane was flipped on its back, killing Koga. This aircraft was eventually recovered by American forces and was rebuilt to fly again, becoming a valuable comparative and training tool when tested against American aircraft.

A photograph reportedly taken shortly after Nishikaichi's crash shows both landing gear and the drop-tank lying next to the fuselage. The flaps are still in their down position. This picture also gives the clearest photographic evidence of the level of battle damage the aircraft sustained. When the photo is blown up, several holes in the rear fuselage and a drop-tank appear to be present. A larger hole near the lower front of the fuselage, just above the leading edge of the wing is also in the location of the fuselage fuel tank. The photo was taken late in the day, the time-lost Niihau resident who took the picture had the sun to his back.

Hawila Kaleohano was standing in the front yard of his house watching a horse's curiously agitated behavior when Nishikaichi's plane slammed down and lurched to a stop less than 30 feet away. After the initial shock of the moment, Kaleohano quickly ran to the fighter and stepped up on its wing. The aircraft was obviously foreign, but like everyone else on remote Niihau, Hawila. had no knowledge of the Japanese attack. Still, its presence was suspicious.

Upon seeing Kalehano, the still-stunned Nishikaichi fumbled for his pistol, but Hawila quickly reached in and took it, before pulling Nishikaichi from the cockpit. In the ensuing action Hawila ripped off a flight suit pocket that contained papers, including a map of Oahu, which he also took.

Hawila Kaleohano then ushered the bewildered pilot toward his house. Nishikaichi had studied enough English in school to awkwardly inquire, "Are you Japanese?" Hawila answered, "No, I am Hawaiian."

Hawila's wife prepared coffee and some food for Nishikaichi. After the pilot had eaten, Hawila and Nishikaichi smoked cigarettes together. Trying to communicate in uneasy English, Nishikaichi tried to get Hawila to return his papers. Kaleohano refused. The lan-

A Niihau resident inspects Nishikaichi's Zero not long after its landing.

guage gap between them made the unusual situation even more difficult. What was a shot up Japanese warplane doing in Hawaii?

Four people of Japanese ancestry would each play a notable role in what followed. Two of the four were contract workers on the island, another was a long-time resident and as well as a Niihau ranch employee. The final one was a U.S. Army Lieutenant posted on Kauai.

Ishimatsu Shintani was a Japanese citizen who had moved to Hawaii around 1900, eventually finding work on Niihau. He married a local woman, had three children, and according to the Robinson family was an industrious and loyal employee; "a good little man, very hard-working and peaceful." Shintani got along well with the local Hawaiians and he worked in the production of honey.

Yoshio Harada and his wife Umeno "Irene" were both U.S. citizens born in the Territory of Hawaii to Japanese parents that had originally come to Hawaii for plantation work. They were both born on Kauai in 1903 and 1905 respectively, and grew up there on plantations. Kauai was mostly an agricultural island, and a large percentage of the field-work population was Japanese. Plantation life combined a uniquely concentrated mix of cultural mores with local and Federal laws that promoted a type of caste system that was difficult to break out from. Both Yoshio and Irene spent time in Japanese

Yoshio Harada

Ishimatsu Shintani in his later years

schools on Kauai as was normal for Japanese immigrant children, allowing plenty of opportunity to practice the Japanese language and learn Japanese traditions within their close-knit community.

Yoshio left Kauai to seek better opportunities in California, but returned to Kauai after seven years to marry Irene. Irene herself had toured Japan for nine months with her mother. Yoshio's parents had already moved back to Japan by the time he and Irene married. The couple settled on Kauai and produced three children.

Aylmer came to need additional help at the ranch, and Yoshio and Irene were recommended for the jobs. After meeting them, he offered both Haradas contract employment on Niihau. Despite Irene's reluctance, Yoshio convinced her that it was a good opportunity to save money that could be used towards an anticipated future move to the U.S. mainland. They passed Aylmer's required health examination, and moved to Niihau in 1939, leaving two of their three children with relatives on Kauai. Initially their jobs included raising bees, running a provision store and caring for Aylmer's elderly ranch manager, John Rennie.

1st Lieutenant Hifuo "Jack" Mizuha was exceptional by any standard. Born on Maui in 1913 to Japanese immigrant parents, his life

Lt. Jack Mizuha

evolved differently from Shintani or the Haradas. He spent part of his early education in a Japanese school, but didn't apply himself towards learning the language. Jack eventually attended the University of Hawaii and through the ROTC became a 2nd Lieutenant in the Army Reserves after graduation. He earned a masters degree from the University of Hawaii in 1936, became a high school teacher on Kauai and formally severed his dual citizenship to Japan. By 1941 he was married with a daughter, and had become a Kauai school principal. Later that same year he was called into active service, promoted to 1st Lieutenant and put in command of Burns Field (now Port Allen airport) on Kauai. Because of anti-Japanese immigrant backlash after the Pearl Harbor attack, Mizuha was demoted to executive officer the day after the raid.

A few days later and no doubt still stinging from his recent demotion, Lt. Mizuha was tasked with an unusual mission. Hawila

Kaeohano and five others had made a daring night-time escape from Niihau in a whale boat to alert Aylmer Robinson and the military authorities that a Japanese pilot, aided by a local *"Nisei"* (an American-born offspring from Japanese immigrant parents) had overcome his guard and was threatening to kill the people of Niihau. Mizuha was to lead a squad to secure the island.

After this mission, Mizuha would eventually become part of the famed 100th Infantry Battalion. Exemplifying the unit's "Purple Heart Battalion" legend, Captain Mizuha was wounded as he sought the source of heavy machine gun fire aimed at his men in Italy. Recovering from his wounds, Mizuha got his law degree, held political office, in 1958 was appointed Hawaii's first Attorney General, and in 1961 was named an Associate Justice of the Hawaiian Supreme Court.

A FATAL ALLIANCE

As Hawila Kaleohano and Nishikaichi struggled to communicate, a growing number of the Niihau populace had gathered around the crashed plane and Kaleohano's nearby house, curious about what was happening. Hawila knew that there were several people on the island who could speak Japanese, so he sent a runner to find his first choice of interpreter, Ishimatsu Shintani.

Shintani arrived with no enthusiasm for the assignment. After a short exchange between himself and Nishikaichi, Shintani appeared even more stressed and quickly departed without relaying any information to the Hawaiians. Keith Robinson would later write that Shintani may have faced the worst dilemma on the island - his Japanese commoner's traditional deference to a member of Japan's respected military class conflicted with loyalties to Aylmer, the Niihau community and his Hawaiian wife and their half-Hawaiian children.

The next potential interpreters to be summoned were Yoshio and Irene Harada. When they arrived, Yoshio and the pilot immediately began conversing. Nishikaichi told them about the Japanese attack on Oahu, and that Hawila had taken his pistol and papers, which he wanted back. The Haradas initially chose to say nothing of the attack to the rest of the islanders.

In the Hawaiian tradition, that evening an impromptu luau was held for their "guest" at Joseph Kele's house. Although it was a friendly event, there was a growing suspicion among the islanders about the nature of the foreign aviator and his shot up plane.

The Niihau residents may have been isolated from the rest of Hawaii, but they were not completely displaced from technology. Some of the residents were enthusiastic photographers, but modern claims that the islanders learned of the Pearl Harbor attack that evening via radio news broadcasts simply aren't supported by their interviews, articles, or the Robinson family history of that time. There were no battery-powered "farm radios" on the island. They did not know that Martial Law had been declared over the entire Territory, or that a curfew and blackout were mandated across the island chain. Ongoing discussions among the islanders finally led to a general consensus; they wanted answers about the real meaning of the aviator's presence. In time, Harada would directly interpret Nishikaichi's words to them. News of the war between Japan and America had come to Niihau.

Nishikaichi was in a tough spot. He was being held on an enemy island, with a growing likelihood of being handed over to U.S. military officials. His weapon, the papers and a map he had used during the attack had already been taken away; his only path to possible escape was the radio in his plane to make contact with the submarine — if it was still nearby. At the same time he needed to destroy the valuable Zero and its secrets before the enemy got their hands on it. Somehow, he would have to find a way...

The following two documents are the most accurate and direct description of the events that happened next. The first report presented here was prepared for Lt. Colonel Fitzgerald, Commander of the Kauai Military District by Lt. Jack Mizuha. Lt. Mizuha compiled the information for his report from interviews during a hearing he held on Niihau on December 14, 1941, a little more than twenty four hours after the tragic conclusion of the episode.

Mizuha's report is remarkable for the detail it gives, the only glaring discrepancy is the time of day stated for the crash of the Zero, about one hour later than Hawila Kaleohano stated. Mizuha's report was based on incidents described by the Niihau residents gathered before him, with the Niihau school teacher Hanna Niheu officiating and Aylmer Robinson aiding in the translations. It must be read carefully: the information is not always presented in a purely sequential format.

The second report was written by U.S. Naval Reserve Lieutenant C.B. Baldwin. This document is complimentary to the Mizuha report, even using the Mizuha report's time of Nishikaichi's crash. It adds significant additional insights, including how Aylmer Robinson and the military authorities were notified of Nishikaichi's presence, the following insurgency, and the mission to secure the island. After explaining the circumstances surrounding the military response, the Baldwin report gives a much more linear and concise overview of the events on Niihau. When combined, the timelines and descriptions of both reports place Mizuha on site as interviews with the Niihau islanders took place.

All following reports are presented here in their original form. The spelling, grammar and punctuation are as originally written. Lt. Mizuha did an admirable job capturing exotically spelled Hawaiian names on paper, but a few minor errors exist. Any mistakes committed to typed reports in those days were not as easily corrected as they are now. Corrections, Hawaiian name spelling errors or notes made by this author appear in parenthesis, in a different font and are italicized. Also, understand that even American born citizens of Japanese ancestry were still generically referred to as Japanese at that time - the title "Japanese-American" hadn't been invented yet.

"The Mizuha Report"

DECLASSIFIED
E.O. 12356 Sec3.3
NND Project 868091

Report of Events Since Sunday, 7 December, 1941 on Niihau.

    The Japanese plane came down near Howard (*Hawila*) Kaleohano's house on Sunday, 7 December, 1941 between 1 and 2 o'clock in the afternoon *(author's note: the estimated time of landing in this report is one hour later than Kaleohano described).* The plane was flying low about 75 yards from Kaleohano's house, apparently out of gasoline, and tried to zoom up again when its undergear got caught in the fence wire and the plane landed flat on the ground. It must have had its landing gear down, because both wheels were knocked off at the time the expedition party arrived at the plane. Howard (*Hawila*) Kaleohano was at home at the time the plane came down and ran with it. He saw that it wasn't an American plane and thought it strange. Upon reaching the cockpit, he saw this Japanese aviator with a pistol in his hand, trying to unstrap his safety belt. Kaleohano immediately grabbed the pistol, taking it away from him, and pulled the aviator out of the cockpit. Kaleohano searched him and took away from him some papers which included an Oahu map. At the time the aviator was in the cockpit, he immediately, perhaps unconsciously thought of his papers and reached for his pocket, which put Kaleohano wise to it, and as a result, Kaleohano searched him outside. By this time the whole populace of Niihau had come to the plane and they decided to keep the aviator at Joseph Kele's house.

The aviator was fet (*fed*) at Kele's house and was guarded there Sunday night. On Monday he was taken to Keei (*correct spelling: Kii - the northeastern most portion of Niihau*), where they planned to send him to Kauai on the Robinson sampan, but it didn't come through. The aviator was brought back and on Tuesday he was again taken to Keei (*Kii*), but the launch did not come in that day. He was kept at Keei (*Kii*) Tuesday night until Wednesday morning. They returned Wednesday afternoon and took him to Yoshio Harada's house. Five men remained to stay on guard at Harada's house.

At the time the aviator was brought to Harada's house, Harada showed no signs of disloyalty, and took his regular turn at guarding the aviator.

On Sunday, when the plane first landed, Shintani, the alien Japanese, had a few words with the aviator, but there wasn't any lengthy conversation.

On Thursday, Harada, the citizen Japanese, asked to have Shintani come down and have Shintani help guard the aviator, as he, Harada, didn't want the entire responsibility being the only Japanese with the aviator, and wanted both to share the responsibility.

John Kekuhina (*John Kekuhina Kaohelaulii was the top foreman on Niihau, pastor of the church and captain of the whale boat*) told Shintani to come down, but Shintani said he didn't want to go that night but would go the following day when his work would be down there near Harada's place. On Friday morning Kekuhina went to Paniau (*the high mountain*) to make a fire as a signal to Kauai. Shintani went on Friday to Harada's house and saw Harada and the aviator. The Hawaiians had no idea what went on among them as they did not understand the language. They do not know how much conversation took place.

At a little after 1 o'clock on the after-

41

noon on Friday, Kaleoao Keale was returning from work and he saw Shintani with the two Japanese at Harada's house, Shintani apparently eating his lunch at the time. About half an hour later, Keale returned and Shintani was through with his lunch and had gone away. Shintani later told Keale that he had gone to his bee apiary to do his work. As far as Keale knows, Shintani didn't see the aviator or the Japanese again.

At about four o'clock in the afternoon, Friday, 12 December 1941, Shintani came to Howard (*Hawila*) Kaleohano's house. Shintani woke Kaleohano up by pounding on the door. Shintani asked Kaleohano if he had the aviator's papers and he replied in the affirmative. Kaleohano showed him first the Oahu map. Shintani replied that it wasn't the Oahu map he wanted. It was the other papers he wanted. Kaleohano went for the other papers and got them out, and whoed (*showed*) them to Shintani. Shintani told him that it meant life and death to Shintani. Kaleohano refused to give the papers. Shintani asked again "Won't you give them to me so I can burn them." Kaleohano refused, saying it was against the law and both of them would be punished if the papers were destroyed. Shintani then offered money which was estimated by Kaleohano to be about $200.00. Shintani was refused again. Shintani repeated again that it was life or death but did not say to whom. Shintani then disappeared from the picture after this.

At about 5:30 Friday afternoon, the aviator and Harada, and a boy, Kalihilihi Niau, about 16 years of age, came to Kaleohano's house. Harada was prodding the boy with a gun. Kaleohano was in the outhouse (*lavatory*) at that time and hid from the Japanese. After looking for Kaleohano for a while, they left the house and went to the plane. It was at this time, it is presumed that

42

the aviator recovered the pistol from Kaleohano's house. Kaleohano left the premises and met
Kaahikili (*Kaahakila*) Kalimahuluhulu and explained
to him the trouble, told him what was going on,
and asked for horses. At the same time another
boy, Naalulu (*Nalulu*) Kanahele (*Kaiwi*) gave him the
horse and Kaleohano gave the alarm that the men
were on the rampage. Before going to the mountains, Kaleohano returned to his house and hid
the aviator's papers in another locality away
from the house, with the exception of the Oahu
map. He then went to another house and got a
pair of shoes and went to the mountains. He got
to Paniau at about 9 o'clock, where some other
men had kerosene lamps with reflectors, signaling
Kauai. They came down after putting out the kerosene lamps and went to Keei (*Kii*). At half past
twelve on Friday night, they left Keei (*Kii*) and
on Saturday afternoon at three o'clock they got
to Waimea (*Kauai*).

The men who put out in the whale *(boat)* to come
to Kauai to sound the alarm were Kekuhina Kaohelaulii, commander of the boat, Howard (*Hawila*)
Kaleohano, Akario (*Akana*) Kaohalaulii (*Kaohelaulii*),
Enoka Kaohelaulii, Billy (*Willy*) Kaohelaulii, and
Kohokuloa (*Kahokuloa*) Kanahele. (*Author's note: Four aboard
the whale boat were brothers, Willie was notorious for sea-sickness. Akana
would replace his brother as foreman of the island when John Kekuhina
retired.*)

Sometime on Friday afternoon the aviator
asked to go out to the toilet at Harada's house.
He asked the guard to go across the yard to the
honey warehouse. Harada then went *(out)* of the
house also. Hanaiki (*Hanaike*) Nihou (*Niheu*), the
husband of the schoolteacher, was the guard at
that time, and he followed the aviator across
the yard followed by Harada. Harada opened the
honey warehouse, and they went in and got Harada's shotgun, and then turned upon the guard

and had him at their mercy. The aviator had the
shotgun in his hand. They went down to the next
warehouse below, opened it and ordered Hanaiki
into it and locked Hanaiki (*Hanaike*) in it. The
rest of the guards were not present as they were
on the committee arranging the work for the next
day. They didn't see any of this.

Mrs. Nihou (*Niheu*) had been living over the
hill from the ranch headquarters where the Haradas live. She was short of supplies and went
down with her children, Keia (*Kia*), Lisa, Mele,
and a little baby. They were returning to the
village in a wagon with Lisa riding the horse
pulligg (*pulling*) the wagon. When they were past the
upper side of the house on the hill road, Keia
(*Kia*) heard Harada calling, Harada ahead and the
aviator following, running down the hill. Harada asked them to stop. Mrs. Nihou (*Niheu*) kept
on going. Harada ran out and told them to stop
the car. Harada stopped the wagon and commanded
everybody to get down from the car, on threat of
their lives. Harada held the gun at Mrs. Nihou's
(*Niheu's*) shoulders but didn't shoot. The two Japanese got into the wagon and called to Loisa (*Lisa?*)
who was told to stay on the horse, to drive fast
with the wagon. They held the gun behind Loisa
(*Lisa?*). They came to the gate at Kaleohano's house
and they left the cart there and went to Kaleohano's house. They picked up the boy at the
airplane whom they were prodding with the gun at
the time Kaleohano saw them. This boy, Kalihilihi, had been guarding the plane in the absence
of his father. By this time, all the people had
the alarm, and they had left the houses and gone
into hiding.

At the end of the village, the two Japa-
nese captured Kalanapie (*Kalanipio*) Niiau (*Niau*) and
the told him to call the other people. They came
down through the village, and under duress, Ni-

iau (*Niau*) was calling for the others. Kaahakila
Kalimahuluhulu was at the house of his relatives trying to get them all out of the way and
got practically every one of them into shelter
and he heard Niiau (*Niau*) calling and he thought
Niiau (*Niau*) was calling for help. So Kalimahuluhulu answered the call. It was dark then, and
when he went out to the road to meet them, Ka-
limahulhulu was also seized as a captive. They
tied Kalimahuluhulu's hands behind him and with
the two captives they came down through the town
calling for the others. Nobody else came. They
came to Joseph Kele's house, where Kalimahul-
hulu saw a light which disappeared suddenly. No
one could be found at Kele's house, so they ordered Niiau (*Niau*) and Kalimahuluhulu to go down
to the gate where they had left the wagon. They
were then ordered to go where the plane was.
Both captives saw that they had taken the cartridges out and had piled them on the wing of
the plane. The aviator went into the plane and
heard him run the radio. He put on his earphones and began calling in Japanese, but the
captives did not hear any reply. They had a big
pile of cartridges and Harada forced Niiau (*Niau*)
to help him carry the cartridges to the wagon.
Then when they came back again, the machine gun
was taken out. Niiau (*Niau*) had to carry it down
to the cart. Harada told Kalimahuluhulu to go to
Keeikia to tell Harada's wife that he won't be
back tonight- that they were going to look for
Kaleohano. Kalimahuluhulu instead of going there
went to the beach and joined his family there.
He got his wife to untie his hands and got Benny
Nokaka (*Benehakaka*) Kanahele who was there to join
him to recover the cartridges Harada had told
him that the cartridges were enough to kill off
every man, woman, and child on the island. Harada and the aviator had gone off looking for the

rest of the people. So Kalimahuluhulu and Benny (*Benehakaka*) came up to the deserted wagon. The machine gun was missing, but the cartridges were there. Kalimahuluhulu took one bunch and Benny (*Benehakaka*) took the other and took them down to the beach and hid them.

Benny (*Benehakaka*) then went to take care of his family, went to get horses to hide his family. Benny (*Benehakaka*) told his family not to tell Harada about his whereabouts. Kalimahuluhulu and Kanahele's family were captured on Saturday morning. They said (*the Japanese*) thatif (*that if*) they could catch Kaleohano, the rest of the people would be let off. If they couldn't, they would kill everybody else.

During Friday night, these two men burned the plane and Kaleohano's house about three o'clock in the morning. They went through the village and shot off the guns on Friday night. (*Author's note: according to subsequent Robinson and Niihau islander interviews, the villagers all fled to the mountains when they heard the gunfire.*)

The Japanese told the families to find Kaleohano. The aviator had recovered the pistol at that time from Kaleohano's house. Harada had the shotgun. The two Japanese started out looking. They said they would kill the two women and then they would kill themselves. Then afterwards they changed their ideas and told Kalimahuluhulu's wife to go into the kea (*koa*) forest to find Kaleohano. She escaped in that fashion.

Bene (*Benehakaka*) Kanahele had been captured along with his family early in the morning. He was sent into the thickets looking for Kaleohano and came back and joined his wife who was held captive. That is when Mr. and Mrs. Kanahele finished off the aviator and Harada killed himself. (*The complete version of this part of the story can be secured from Mr. and Mrs. Kanahele who were not questioned at Niihau, but were brought back to Kauai.)* The guns were not recovered as they were hidden by the native in the kea (*koa*) forest and could not be found by them. Mr. Elmer (*Aylmer*) Robinson left instructions with the natives to make a diligent search for the guns, which if recovered would be turned over to him and then turned over to the military commander of the Kauai District.

The above story was repeated to the undersigned officer by Mr. Elmer (*Aylmer*) Robinson who secured the story from the various natives in the village. Mr. Robinson secured the story in Hawaiian and translated it into English. The English version was taken down by this officer by stenographic notes.

Captain Eugene MacManus, harbormaster at Port Allen, was present during this entire hearing.

Jack H. Mizuha
1st Lt., 299th Infantry

"The Baldwin Report"

```
Received          FOURTEENTH NAVAL DISTRICT
12/19/41          Branch Intelligence Office
Dist. Intell.     Port Allen, Kauai, T.H.     CBB/
on
```

```
CONFIDENTIAL                    December 16, 1941
```

```
From:       Officer-in-Charge, Zone 4.
To:         District Intelligence Officer.
```

```
Subject:    Crash of Enemy Plane on Niihau.
Enclosure:  Copy of Lieut. Jack Mizuha's re
            port on same subject, to Lt. Col.
            Fitzgerald, Commanding Officer,
            Kauai Military District.
```

1.   On Saturday, December 13, 1941 at 3:00 P.M. , six Niihau Hawaiians, captained by Kekuhina Kaohelaulii, landed at Waimea, Hawaii in a whale boat, to report to the Robinson family of Makaweli, Kauai, T.H., the crash of a Japanese plane on Niihau. The crew left Niihau that same day at 12:30 A.M., and rowed to Kauai, making the trip in about fifteen hours.

2.   Lt. Colonel Fitzgerald was notified and immediately organized an expedition squad of twelve armed soldiers from Company "M", 299th Infantry under the supervision of Lieut. Jack Mizuha of the same Company. The lighthouse tender "Kukui" fortunately was at Niihau extinguishing lighthouse lights. A dispatch was sent to havd *(have)* it return to Waimea, Kauai, immediately to take the above named troops to Niihau.

3.   The "Kukui", having about twelve armed
men of its own and two machine guns, left Waimea
at about six P. M. Saturday December 13, 1941,
and arrived at southwest point, Keanapuka, Niihau, as Nonopapa, the main landing, was too
rough. The party Of armed soldiers went ashore
Sunday about 7:30 A.M., and had breakfast, then
had to walk about ten miles to the Nonopapa village, where the plane crashed nearby, arriving
there at 1:50 P.M.

4.   When the troops reached the village and plane, they found that there was only
one plane and one Japanese pilot, who had already been killed and buried. The plane had been
burned by the pilot at three A.M. Saturday morning, December 13, 1941.

5.   The description of the plane is as
follows: The Japanese plane, burned by the pilot, had its fuselage burned but the wings, tail
and engine were intact. It had a three-blade
propeller which was bent. The plane was small,
possibly twenty feet long, and twenty feet from
wing tip to wing tip, but sturdy and made of
metal, probably of magnesium and not aluminum.
It was a fighter type with four 20mm cannons, one
in each wing, and two, either in the propeller
hub and synchronized with the engine or in the
cockpit. Single engine, average size, possibly
Curtiss-Wright engine, and had a G. E. generator, An American radio set,(make unknown) which
was damaged by the fire.

6.   Rising-Sun insignia on each wing
tip, top and bottom. The number of the plane, on
the tail was BII-120. Both landing wheels were
severely damaged.

7.　　　The complete details of the entire
episode of the crash, as explained to Officer-in-
Charge, by Mr. Elmer *(Aylmer)* Robinson and Benny
(Benehakaka) Kanahele, now in Waimea, Kauai, Hospital, from December 7 to 14, inclusive is explained herein. Please note that this report is
more brief and concise than the enclosed report
to the Army. Mr. Elmer *(Aylmer)* Robinson stated
that the picture given to this office was his
compiled story of the various day-by-day incidents, and that the report made by Lieut. Jack
Mizuha included the remarks made by a large
gathering of Hawaiians at a meeting held on
Niihau, Sunday at 3 PM December 14, 1941. This
meeting was conducted by Mr. Elmer *(Aylmer)* Robinson, as he speaks Hawaiian fluently. Questions
and answers were made in Hawaiian and translated
into English.

8.　　　Sunday between 1 and 2 P.M. December
7, 1941, at Niihau, various Hawaiian residents
of the island saw two planes flying over Niihau.
One crashed quite close to the Nonopapa village
and the other flew on west, past the island and
presumably crashed in the sea. However, it was
never seen again. Incidentally, the residents of
the island had absolutely no means of communication with Kauai or elsewhere and were unaware of
the United States being at war with Japan. Mr.
Elmer *(Aylmer)* Robinson wrote a letter about December 9, 1941, informing the Niihau population that
the United States was at war, but unfortunately
it was not delivered by a detailed sampan.

9.　　　The single-seater fighter plane only
had one Japanese pilot who was seized by the Hawaiians immediately after it crashed into a fence
next to the village, and before the pilot could
locate his pistol. Then Howard *(Hawila)* Kaleohano

50

searched the plane and secured all the papers, map of Oahu, and pistol for safekeeping, to be turned over to the proper source ultimately.

10.   The pilot surrendered before all the Hawaiians and remained peaceful and friendly and lived at the village and at first was not kept in custody, but was allowed to roam about unguarded. At first, when spoken to, he would reply in English writing, then later spoke English to the Hawaiians fluently . He was possibly educated on the mainland.

11.   Then on Tuesday he was placed under guard of Harada and Shintani, and was sent to Kii, furtherest northeast end of Niihau, hoping to send the pilot to Kauai by sampan or Robinson's whale boat that was stationed there in their boat house. As the sea was too rough, he was returned to the village and again another trip was made to Kii on Wednesday, but was returned a second time on account of bad weather.

-2-

subject: Crash of Enemy Plane on Niihau.

12.   Thursday Harada complained to the Hawaiians, stating that it was a mistake that the two Niihau Japanese were selected as guards for the pilot. They were then relieved of their duty, and later in the day, Harada, the citizen, asked a Hawaiian to have Shintani, the alien, come and see him, to discuss some matters, but Shintani wouldn't come.

13.   Then on Friday Shintani had lunch with the Hawaiians. After the Hawaiians were through *(with)* work, Shintani went to Howard *(Hawila)* Kaleohano's house at the village and asked for the papers . Howard *(Hawila)* was guarding the plane nearby. Howard *(Hawila)* Kaleohano obtained the map then Shintaini said- not that, but the other papers so he could burn and destroy them.

14.   Then Shintani produced about $200.00 in an attempt to bribe Howard *(Hawila)* Kaleohano . He refused the bribe at first and more so after the money was offered for the papers. Then Shintani said excitedly that it was a matter of death or   life, and insisted that Japan made him do this. After this, Shintani disappeared out of the picture entirely.

15.   Friday night, Harada and pilot broke into Shintani's house looking for the papers. As Shintani had joined the Hawaiians, they failed to secure the papers. Harada and the pilot then became furious, and seeing Shintani in the village later, then chased him but he got away. Then some of the Hawaiians were taken prisoners by Harada and the pilot and tied up – the other Hawaiians were away from the village. After Shintani left the village, the pilot asked Harada if he had another gun. Earlier in the day Harada and the pilot had been to Kaleohano's house and presumably had found the pilot's pistol during Kaleohano's absence, but felt that each should have a weapon with which to control their Hawaiian prisoners. Then Harada took the pilot to the honey house which was close to the village, and got a shotgun and some cartridges.

16.   About midnight the pilot attempted to send a message from his radio in the plane, in

Japanese. A few of the Hawaiians heard him talking, but did not hear a reply. The residents,
knowing he had sent the message, were aware at
this time that there was a war on, and became
alarmed, as they were afraid the pilot had sent
for aid from the enemy. The pilot burned his
plane at 3 A.M.

Saturday, December 13, 1941. At the same time,
he burned Kaleohanos' house, hoping to destroy
his map and papers which he thought to be hidden
there.

17.   The Hawaiians at the village were
well scattered. Some went to the top of the
mountain with kerosene lamps and reflectors and
attempted to signal Kauai.

-3-

Subject: Crash of Enemy Plane on Niihau.

Some were at the beach, while some Hawaiians
were riding from the mountains to Kii beach to
prepare the whale boat for a trip to Kauai.
While the pilot was at the plane before burning
it, the Hawaiian
had the pilot's papers at the mountain top,
and later took them to Kii. Six strong Hawaiians left Kii in the whale boat at 12:30 A.M.
Saturday , December 13, 1941, for Kauai, arriving about fifteen hours Later, at Waimea, Kauai,
at 8:00 P.M. They reported to the Robinsons at
Makaweli, Kauai.

18.   That night the Hawaiians on Niihau
had a prayer meeting then all left for the mountains to join the others who were already there.

A few stragglers were captured by the pilot and Harada who said they would be released if they told them where the papers were. They also had two machine guns with them which had been taken from the plane in the afternoon. Shintani never at any time had any firearms and was not implicated in the case except for attempting to bribe the Hawaiian as previously mentioned.

19.   Saturday, December 13,1941 at 10:00 A.M., Benny *(Benehakaka)* Kana-hele attempted to grab the pilot's pistol but failed. They *(Then)* Benny's *(Benehakaka's)* wife who was next to him, grabbed the pistol and Harada pulled her away. Then the pilot, still having the pistol, shot Benny *(Benehakaka)* three times, in the right and lift thighs and on his upper right side. All were flesh wounds.

20.   Benny *(Benehakaka)* Kanahele then picked up the pilot bodily and dashed his head on a stone wall and killed him. Harada then shot himself in the abdomen twice and died soon afterward. The bodies were temporarily buried at Niihau away from the village.

21.   The Kauai Army expedition party arrived as stated at 1:50 P.M. Sunday December 14, 1941 at the village. They returned to Port Allen, Kauai on the "Kukui" , arriving about 7:30 A.M. Monday tDecember 15, 1941. Shintani , Mrs. Harada and her child were brought back and were imprisoned under Colonel Fitzgerald's control. Benny *(Benehakaka)* Kanahele, the wounded man, is now in the hospital at Waimea, Kauai.

C. B. BALDWIN
Lieut. U.S.N.R.

54

We don't know the details of the private discussions between Nishickaichi, Shintani and the Haradas during their time together in those first days after the pilot's crash on Niihau. Certainly Nishikaichi was desperate to find an ally, and the Haradas would eventually prove sympathetic to his situation. Was the pilot able to convince them of Japan's inevitable dominance over Hawaii or America? What we do know is that once Yoshio Harada committed himself to help Nishikaichi, there was no going back. The Haradas had woven themselves into the fabric of life on Niihau since moving to the island, and in joining the pilot's cause, Yoshio turned on his neighbors and co-workers in an unapologetic fashion.

The real point of no return for Yoshio Harada was when he took Aylmer Robinson's personal shotgun from the Robinson ranch house, and then hid it in the honey warehouse near the Harada home. The elderly ranch manager that had lived in the ranch house had died earlier that year, but the Haradas were still granted limited access to the house while Aylmer was on Kauai. Aylmer had his own private room in the ranch house, which was off-limits to all the Niihau islanders, including the Haradas. Aylmer's shotgun, which was kept in his room, was normally the only firearm on the island. From both the Robinson's and the Niihau Hawaiian's perspective, Yoshio stole the weapon.

Although neither report describes how the shotgun came to be in the honey warehouse, further interviews with the Robinsons and the Niihau people confirm where the shotgun came from. The Mizuha

The Robinson ranch house on Niihau.   Photo: Moroz Collection

The honey warehouse today.

report accurately describes the end result of the shotgun's presence in the warehouse — once Harada and Nishikaichi were able to lure the pilot's guard into the warehouse, they were able to overpower him with the weapon, starting the insurgency.

The Baldwin report's singular failing is that it fumbles the shotgun issue in paragraph 15. Baldwin was never on Niihau as Mizuha had been, and a large portion of his report was centered on details of the story that had happened on Kauai where he was stationed. Although Baldwin also interviewed both Aylmer and Bene "Benny" Kanahele after the "*Kukui*" had brought them to Kauai, this one segment of his report proved to be uncharacteristically inaccurate.

George C. Larsen was temporarily aboard *Kukui* as an extra radio operator during the mission to Niihau. Later in life he wrote of his wartime experiences in *"Pearl Harbor: A Memoir of Service."* His description of the trip gives additional interesting insights.

"While in Port Allen the Army requested us to help them recapture Niihau Island, as a Japanese fighter pilot had crashed on the Island and had taken control of the natives with the help of two Japanese workers. So we went over to Niihau Island, arriving a little after dusk with a squad of Army raiders and four of the ship's crew ready to jump ashore for the rescue, they were all armed to the teeth and ready to go. One of the men was my radio partner, an ex-Marine, I wisely volunteered to man the radio shack on board the ship. They came back about midnight with the pilot's belongings. They assembled in the radio shack, as this was the best quarters on the ship to discuss what they accomplished and to view what they found."

"They told us that the pilot was dead. That he was killed by a Hawaiian, who started to grapple with the pilot, who was holding a pistol point-blank range. The pilot fired his pistol three times hitting the native in the groin, thus enraging the Hawaiian who grabbed around the waist and turned him upside down and smashed his head into the ground killing him instantly. The Hawaiian was a 6-foot 6-inch giant and the three shots to the groin apparently didn't affect him that much. They end the story by telling us that his wife took out a knife and cut both of the pilot's ears off. We then got to inspect all the items they brought back with them. First, there was the synchronized machine gun from the fighter plane, then the fish skin water proof wrapping that the pilot had wrapped around his waist containing things like a high school student body card from a local Oahu High School, local maps, money and things necessary if he had to bail out over Oahu. The machine gun still had about twenty bullets hanging from the breach of the gun. I snapped one of the cartridges from the belt figuring it would be an easy souvenir to keep, which it was, (I gave it to the Kauai Museum on January 10, 1991). I asked where was the pilot and they told me that the wounded Hawaiian they brought aboard had killed him and that the natives were going to bury him on the Island. They thought that the stuff they took from him would be enough to verify that he had been taken care of. One of the Japanese servants committed suicide and the other one wasn't helping the pilot as he was forced to help them. The Hawaiian walked on board the ship and when we got back to

Port Allen he insisted on walking from the ship to the ambulance, even though he had three bullets in his groin, he was one tough native."

Was the American currency found among Nishikaichi's belongings the money that Shintani had offered Hawila Kaleohano for the return of the pilot's papers? Sadly, the answer to that question is now lost to history. Modern interviews with the Robinson family describe Shintani as a thrifty and careful man who had become so distressed with Nishikaichi's potential for harm that he likely offered his own precious savings in an effort to ease the tension.

U.S. Coast Guard Lighthouse Tender Kukui.   Photo: National Archives

Benehakaka Kanahele, and his wife were both transported aboard *Kukui* to Kauai so he could receive proper medical attention. Shintani, Irene Harada and her daughter had also been rounded up and put aboard the ship, en route to an uncertain future. Although Irene had not played a physical role in the uprising, her inaction to stop Yoshio or warn the other Niihau residents implied that she was an accessory to her husband's actions.

Benehakaka Kanahele (right) and his wife Ella at the Waimea Hospital.
Photo: National Park Service

The Waimea (Kauai) Hospital Summary records for "Benny Hakata" Kanahele state that the 51 year old was admitted at 8:10 am on December 15, 1941 with gunshot wounds to the left chest wall, left hip and penis. Fortunately, all of the small caliber bullets passed through without causing serious damage. He was discharged from the hospital just 16 days later [13]. Benny and his wife Ella returned to Niihau.

Both Shintani and Irene Harada were temporarily housed in Waimea jail. Irene's daughter was given to Irene's sister who was already taking care of her other two children. There was suspicion amongst the military authorities that Irene might have been a spy: less than a week after she and Shintani had been brought to the jail they began interrogating her. She was stoic and uncooperative, not even giving them Nishikaichi's name. Irene accepted no responsibility for the events on Niihau, and initially showed her defiance at being held against her will by refusing to eat.

What happened to the papers and map that Nishikaichi and

13   Waimea Hospital records

The Niihau whale boat.   Photo: National Park Service

Yoshio Harada had tried so hard to reclaim? Mizuha states that Hawila Kaleohano removed the papers from his house (except for the Oahu map) and moved them to another location. Baldwin wrote that "the Hawaiian" (presumed to be Hawila Kaleohano in this context), brought them to the mountain top and later to Kii. After that there is no direct mention of the documents again. Since Kaleohano and the rest of his party departed from Kii, in the whale boat for Kauai, there is a real likelihood that the papers made the trip with them.

Unfortunately, Nishikaichi's papers have subsequently fallen into the cracks of time, but a relevant alternative still exists which may give some insights as to the type of information that his documents included.

Lieutenant Junior Grade Yoshikazu Saito flew a Nakijima B5N2 "Kate" bomber in the second wave attack on Oahu. He was based on the carrier *Zuikaku* and flew his approach to Oahu in the same massed flight with Nishikaichi. Unlike the single seat Zero fighters,

Lt. Yoshikazu Saito and his "Kate" bomber.   Photo: Saito Family Collection

Saito's plane had three crew members, including a navigator. Saito's navigator produced an attack map of the operation, which survived the war.

The map is a remarkable document, which gives many details about the weather conditions, heading, altitude, times, approach and departure for the second wave. Saito's assigned target was

Hickam Field near Pearl Harbor, but his planned flight path to and from Oahu would have mirrored Nishikaichi's.

All times listed on the attack map are expressed in Tokyo Time as was the standard for all operations of the Japanese Imperial Navy. Saito himself was also briefed on Niihau as an option if he couldn't return to his carrier, but this apparently didn't apply to all airmen involved in the Oahu raid. Years after the war Saito told his son that any flight leader, or second in command who couldn't make it back

Saito's Second Wave Attack Map

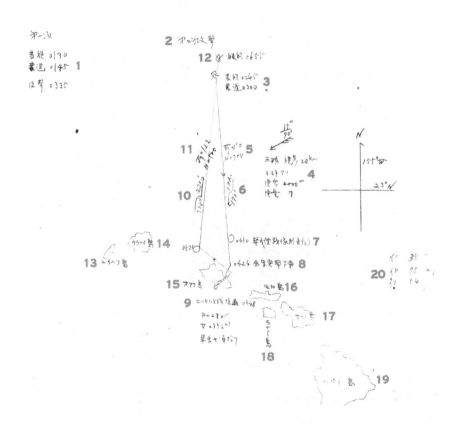

to the fleet was ordered to find an American target and dive into it. A Niihau attempted landing was only for those of lesser rank — if captured, they would have less information to give to the enemy.

Nishikaichi and Harada could not know that a total of 29 Japanese planes had been shot down by the American defenders, and many of those wrecks had been recovered. The documents carried by those downed aircrews were already being scrutinized by military intelligence, as were the remains of their aircraft. Since du-

Map Key

1. The first (attack wave)
   Launch 0130
   Departure 0145
   Attack 0335

2. Second attack (wave)

3. Launch time 0245
   Departure time 0300

4. (Wind) 15 m/sec (33.5 mph)
   70 deg. (from)
   Half clear   visibility 20 km
   Mist
   Ceiling 2000 m
   Cloudiness: 7

5. 150 kts (airspeed)
   300 m (altitude)

6. 170/175 degrees (heading)

7. 0410 Caution zone - time to form
   defense formation for dogfight

8. 0424 All units attack

9. Hickam Air Field bombing 0448
   (altitude) 2800 m
   (speed) 152 kts
   (?) 7 bomb drop

10. Unintelligible

11. (airspeed) 122 kts
    (altitude) 500 m

12. Friendly ship (return to own ship)

13. Nihafu (H) Island (Niihau Island)

14. Kauai Island

15. Oahu Island

16. Molo Island (Molokai Island)

17. Maui Island

18. Lanai Island

19. Hawaii Island

20. FC 35
    FB 78 = 167
    FO 54

Note: All times indicated are Tokyo time

63

plicate information had already been recovered by the Americans, Nishikaichi's papers had little actual military value.

Author Dan King was fortunate to obtain a rare, late-in-life interview with a surviving participant of the Pearl Harbor Raid who knew Nishikaichi. Haruo Yoshino was an observer/navigator in a Nakijima B5N2 "Kate" torpedo bomber that attacked Pearl Harbor's Battleship Row during the first wave. Yoshino's comments in King's book, "*The Last Zero Fighter,*"(*Pacific Press)* give additional perspective to Nihsikaichi's actions from a fellow Japanese airman's point of view.

"Nishikaichi and I went through *Yokaren* (naval aviation preparatory aviation class) together before he went on to become a pilot, and I went to *teisatsu'in* (advanced navigation, gunnery, and bombing) school. I learned after the war he suffered hits to his fuel tanks and crash landed on Niihau Island."

"We were told that if we had trouble to land on the southern shoreline so the rescue sub could see the plane on the beach and come in. There was a submarine, waiting off the coast of Niihau, waiting to pick up any aviators whose planes were damaged. Nishikaichi didn't land his crippled Zero on the beach as instructed, but in the middle of the island in a field. He was out of view. The submarine commander must have scanned the shoreline with the periscope, and seeing no downed aircraft departed the area after the attack."

"Nishikaichi should have killed himself when he realized he missed the rescue window. It was the greatest shame to become a captive. He chose to live, and even harmed innocent civilians. His actions brought dishonor on all of us."

The Territory of Hawaii and the rest of the United States barely had time to digest the reality of the Pearl Harbor attack when the news broke on the events on Niihau. The *Kauai Garden Island War Daily* first broke the news of Hawila Kaleohano's report to Aylmer on December 15, shortly after he and the others had rowed over from Niihau to spread the alarm. Both the *Honolulu Advertiser* and the *Star Bulletin* published articles detailing the story on December 16, 1941. The *Honolulu Advertiser* added a follow-up story on Dec.

19 entitled "Niihau Story Revealed in First Official Version." Radio broadcasts about the incident helped spread the word.

What was left of Nishikaichi's Zero was next to receive attention. Both the Army and later the Navy sent teams to inspect the wreckage and harvest any components that looked to have intelligence value. Expert amateur photographer and Robinson family friend Reverend Paul Denise (pronounced Dee-nice) of Kauai joined the army team (reportedly with a temporary commission and wearing an Army uniform) to document the aircraft as they found it. He took over 500 photos of the Zero and its disassembly.

Other shot-down Japanese aircraft wrecks had already been recovered in various states of condition from crash sites around Oahu. They had been taken to engineering hangars at Hickam and Ford Island for technical evaluation. The distantly located, burned-out remains of Nishikaichi's Zero now offered little that hadn't already been gleaned from more readily accessible crash sites near Oahu's military installations.

Army team lead by Joseph Craco (left) prior to boarding "Lehua" for Niihau
Photo: National Park Service 539.15

One of the first photos Rev. Denise took of Nishikaichi's burnt-out Zero. The hillside trees in the background and the position of the fence line enabled the location of this exact spot to be re-established over 60 years later. Cattle had cropped Niihau's vegetation close to the ground.   Photo: Craig Barnum Collection

*An American-made Bendix Eclipse
generator was found installed on
Nishikaichi's Zero. Other components
such as the propeller, brakes, instruments and radio equipment were
license-built from American companies.
Photo: Craig Barnum Collection*

*The torn off left landing gear.
Photo: Craig Barnum Collection*

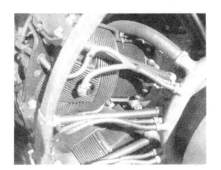

*The Nakajima Sakae 12 engine showed
no battle damage.
Photo: Craig Barnum Collection*

Above: The wing skin and access panels on the right wing have been crudely cut away to expose the 20mm cannon. The haste in which the Army investigative team worked is highlighted by the torn back leading edge panel — instead of simply removing the screws, the metal was cut. On the inside of this panel (lying against the ground) is a faintly visible stencil with the aircraft's serial number.
Photo: Craig Barnum Collection

Left: The fabric covered rudder and elevator already show signs of souvenir collecting. The "20" on this side of the rudder has been cut out as well as the stencil on the bottom of the elevator which displayed the aircraft's serial number. The tail wheel is still in the down position, unaffected by the crash. The tail hook used for carrier landings was located forward of the tail wheel, retracted into a channel in the bottom of the fuselage.
Photo: Craig Barnum Collection

Left: The spinner has been cut off to expose the propeller hub and counterweights. The channel in the top of the cowling is one of two allowing clearance for the bullets from machine guns mounted just forward of the cockpit. These were the guns Nishikaichi and Harada removed before the airplane was burned. The stencil painted on the engine cowl indicated fuel, oil and service information, as well as the name of the person who was who was responsible for it; Service Petty Officer 3rd Class Akimoto.
Photo: Craig Barnum Collection

Below: The aluminum skin from the rear portion left wing has been cut and torn away, exposing the flap actuator and other structural components. This is another example of how quickly the Army team worked to gather intelligence from the wreckage, taking little care to preserve what was left of the Zero.
Photo: Craig Barnum Collection

A 20mm cannon has been removed from the Zero's wing, ready to be taken back to Oahu. These lethal weapons were so powerful that they required substantial structural enhancements to the Zero's lightly built wing. Their explosive shells were devastating to other aircraft.   Photo: Craig Barnum Collection

The remains of the Zero were pulled apart during the Army's investigation, at this point the right wing is missing, the upper engine cowling has been removed, a burned-out section of the cockpit has been dragged to the side and the left wing has been pulled forward. Pieces of the spinner lie in the foreground.
Photo: Craig Barnum Collection

In the confusion after the Pearl Harbor raid, there were heightened fears that the Japanese forces were going to return soon for another attack or perhaps even invade Hawaii. The Army only removed components from the Zero, and had no immediate need to take what was left. There was some concern that if the Japanese returned, the openly exposed fighter's remains might be bombed, destroying the possibility of further study. The decision was made to hide the remnants in a stand of trees, about 200 yards down-slope from the crash site. The Zero's dissected carcass was dragged into the concealing shadows of the trees.

Above: A sailor, part of the Navy's latest investigation team, surveys Nishikaichi's Zero where it was hidden in the shady grove after the Army's own investigation.
Photo: Robinson Collection

Left: Aylmer Robinson photographed aboard the Robinson sampan "Lehua" en route to Niihau with the Army investigative team. He is wearing an uncharacteristic white shirt, attire, he normally wore only on Sundays.
Photo: Robinson Collection

One of the Zero's wings, note how souvenir hunters have already removed much of the metal from the red "meat ball" national marking area on the right.
Photo: Robinson Collection

Above: Soldiers and Niihau islanders gathered at the Puukole landing area on northern Niihau.   Photo: Robinson Collection

The direction of the war had not come completely in focus yet for the American military. The authorities told the Niihau islanders to not talk about the Zero or the incident to anyone. For a time, a small group of soldiers were posted on Niihau. They were ordered to avoid interaction with the native Hawaiians. With little else to do with their free time, they picked at the Zero's remains for souvenirs. When the soldiers left, the Hawaiians peeled off strips of aluminum from the Zero for use in making their fishing nets.

The Mizuha and Baldwin reports triggered additional military analysis in the intelligence community. On January 26, 1942 Captain Mayfield submitted an investigation report as follows...

Period covered: 16 Dec., 1941; 26 Jan.,1942
Status of Case: Closed
Origin of Case: Fourteenth Naval District

United States Naval Intelligence Service

INVESTIGATION REPORT
Confidential
Date: 26 Jan. 1942
Subject: JAPANESE RESIDENTS OF THE T.H. —LOYALTY
OF
Report made at: T.H.
Report made by: C.B. Baldwin, Lt., I-V (S) USNR;
R.W. Breed, End., I-V (S), USNR.

Source File No.: 14ND #1798
ONI File No.:
SYNOPSIS: Report predicated upon Japanese plane
crash on 7 December, 1941, and events subsequent thereto, on Island of Niihau, T. H.

Niihau is one of the smallest Hawaiian Islands,
its meager population consisting mostly of Hawaiians and a few Japanese engaged in cattle
raising, and communications with other islands
nil except by boat. Thus the residents of Niihau had no cognizance of the Japanese attack,
or its extent or effect, until several days after it took place. Pilot of this plane survived
and was taken prisoner by local Hawaiians, who
confiscated his sidearm and flight papers. Among
guards of the aviator were an American-born Japanese named Harada and an alien Japanese named
Shintani, neither of whom had ever been considered disloyal to the United States. Shintani attempted unsuccessfully to secure the possession
of the pilot's papers by bribery, stating it was
a matter of life and death, and that Japan had

forced him to take this action. Shintani, however-
er, later repented and re-joined the Hawaiians.
With the aid of Harada, the pilot recovered his
pistol and a shotgun, set up two machine guns
from his plane, and dominated the island. Pilot
was finally killed by an audacious Hawaiian couple, and Harada committed suicide. Shintani is
now in custodial detention.

DEDUCTIONS: The fact that the two Niihau Japanese who had previously shown no anti- American tendencies went to the aid of pilot when
Japanese domination of the island seemed possible, indicates likelihood that Japanese residents previously believed loyal to the United
States, may aid Japan if further Japanese attacks appear successful.
  CLOSED
  RWB/zw
  Approved :

MAYFIELD,
Captain, U.S. Navy,
District Intelligence Officer.

 The news had spread nationally about the happenings on Niihau. A song commemorating the event was composed by Hawaiian composer Alexander Anderson, titled "They Couldn't Take Niihau No-How" (see appendix 1). Hawila Kaleohano was paid for his financial losses by the Army, and for a time bathed in the glow of celebrity. The unusual story had brought Niihau quickly, but only briefly into the national conscience.

 The rapid-fire evolution of the war in the Pacific as well as in Europe quickly eclipsed the Forbidden Island's events. Other news-worthy developments captured America's attention. Now consid-ered an enemy alien, Shintani was shipped to the U.S. mainland for internment. He would write pathetic letters to Aylmer, begging to be allowed to resume his Niihau existence. Irene Harada was transferred to other facilities on Kauai and Oahu before ending up in an internment camp in Honouliuli, Oahu.

Irene was a U.S. citizen, and if she was also sent to the mainland there was a possibility that she might be released. Because of the special nature of her case, she was kept on Oahu in a camp that held Japanese, German, and Italian nationals as well as the captured commander of a Japanese mini- sub that had accidentally run aground at Bellows during the Pearl Harbor attack.

Irene was still the subject of occasional interrogations by the FBI during this phase of her confinement. Her earlier sightseeing trip to Japan with her mother was a marker for the agents, and they still questioned her about being a spy. She denied the accusations, and continued to be stubbornly elusive about information regarding the events on Niihau.

The pendulum of the Pacific War would eventually swing in America's favor, and the need for martial law in Hawaii began to be challenged. This relaxation affected the detainees as well. Irene wrote a letter in October, 1943 to Lt. Col Slattery of the Military Intelligence Division, proclaiming her innocence, describing her suffering and her desire to be reunited with her children [14]. Although Slattery recommended a rehearing, the Military Governor's Review Board denied it. She would gain her freedom eight months later, after signing a statement releasing the government from any legal responsibility stemming from her arrest and internment.

Irene went to see Aylmer shortly after her release, hoping to acquire items she felt had been unaccounted for during her unplanned departure from Niihau and subsequent internment. The visit was unsuccessful; Aylmer's perspective was that he had already financially squared with her for her work on the island, and that her presence was no longer appropriate. After the ordeal on Niihau, both Aylmer and the Niihau islanders considered her *persona non grata*. Keith Robinson would later write

14   The Niihau Incident A. Beekman page 99-100 Heritage press of the Pacific

that for decades after the event, many Niihau islanders insisted that Irene had quietly done things to help the Japanese side.

Aylmer's dismissal of Irene has been reinterpreted by some in the 21st century as a manifestation of racial prejudice. A lesser known fact is that Shintani was happily welcomed back by Aylmer after his release, and spent the rest of his life working on Niihau. He would become the progenitor of the mostly-Hawaiian (but Japanese named) Shintani family of Niihau and west Kauai.

Irene was rejoined with her children in Kapaa, Kauai. On July 18, 1944 she wrote to Kiyoshi Yamamoto, who was still in confinement with his family in the Honouliuli internment camp. The four page, handwritten letter was newsy and friendly, but does give some insight as to her frame of mind at the time of her release. "It is real something to obtain freedom again and to be in the civilization. Although I still feel pessimistic with the community as I hardly go out where crowds are. The least I talk the better I feel. With the tragedy, the wound was so deep, its hard to hide my pain in my heart so I try hard to keep away from people, however- I will have to do something in near future although I haven't decided what I should do." Irene would eventually open a sewing shop in Kapaa, on the opposite side of Kauai from Niihau.

With the war over and the soldiers gone, Niihau reverted back into the isolated ranch it had been before. Keeping true to the instructions they were given by the military in 1941, neither the islanders nor the Robinsons spoke of the Zero to outsiders. The details of the Nishikaichi and Harada story were kept alive as part of the lore of the island's people and the Robinson family, but rarely discussed beyond their own cloistered domain.

Over ten years after the event, Irene was still a person of interest-this time from the Japanese. In the summer of 1953, Mitsuo Fuchida, the commander of the attack on Pearl Harbor, would meet with Irene on Kauai.

During planning for the attack, it had been Fuchida's concept to use Niihau as an emergency airfield for damaged Japanese airplanes. A submarine could be posted in the deep water just offshore west of the island to pick up any downed aircrews. He proposed the idea to Lt. Commander Minoru Genda, the Operations Staff Officer of the First Aviation Fleet, who then passed it on to the Combined Fleet's Command Center for approval. They agreed, and ordered the Sixth Fleet to dispatch a submarine to Niihau for duty on the day of the raid.

After the war Fuchida's own life had taken an unusual twist. By chance he had run into ex-Doolittle Raider and POW Jacob DeShazer who was evangelizing at a Tokyo train station in 1949. A pamphlet that DeShazer gave Fuchida eventually led to Fuchida converting to Christianity and becoming an evangelist himself.

In 1953 Fuchida had stopped in Hawaii to evangelize before returning to Japan after completing a lengthy religious tour of the U.S. After arriving on Kauai, he received an anonymous letter from someone in Honolulu that praised his success during the Pearl Harbor raid and stated that a Japanese Petty Officer had crashed on the island of "Nihahu" (Niihau) and was buried there. The unknown writer added "Please make sure to go to Nihahu (Niihau) Island to visit the grave. It is your great responsibility as the commander."

Fuchida had not been aware of Nishikaichi's end on Niihau until the letter. Through friends on Kauai he found out the island was privately owned by the Robinson family. He contacted Aylmer, who granted Fuchida a brief visit to Niihau, traveling aboard a vessel that was to pick up some cattle from the island. For the first time, Fuchida learned some of the details of the Japanese aviator/Harada story.

Immediately after returning from Niihau, Fuchida visited Irene Harada in Kapaa, Kauai. Since he now knew the Japanese pilot's fate, Irene talked to him openly about the aviator, and identified him as Shigenori Nishikaichi, something she had successfully resisted when questioned by U.S. officials. Because of the misfortune brought to Mrs. Harada and her children by the war, Fuchida offered his sincere apology. He wrote her reply in his memoir; "I am puzzled you apologize so much. There is nothing wrong for the U.S. military authority to have convicted me for treason, as I am an American citizen born in the United States. However, under our skin, the blood that flows is Japanese. Therefore, I do not think that my husband did anything wrong." [15]

In 1959, Japanese Vice Consul Takegoro Sato came to Kauai to interview Irene about the Niihau affair. As with Fuchida, her elevated comfort level with Sato resulted in her confirming to the Vice Council the identity of the crashed Japanese aviator on Niihau as being Shigenori Nishikaichi.

Author Allan Beekman found it more difficult to capture and retain her trust. He tried to gain her perspective for three articles about Niihau he wrote in the early 1970s for a Tokyo magazine and a Japanese American Citizen's League publication. By the time he was finishing his book *"The Niihau Incident"* in 1982, she had become progressively less cooperative. In the end, his efforts to engage her faltered; Irene's increasingly defensive attitude left him with little additional insight [16].

Irene was much less reserved during her final interview for a Japanese audience. She and Yoshio were perceived in Japan to have performed a heroic act; helping a brave and understandably desperate Japanese airman trapped on enemy soil. Because of growing interest about the Niihau story, a Japanese film crew was sent to Kauai to interview Irene for a television program to be broadcast in Japan on the 50th anniversary of the Pearl Harbor attack. Part of Irene's understanding in agreeing to do the interview was it would never be presented outside of Japan. The Tokyo Broadcasting Station broadcast *"A Woman Who Was Called A Spy"* as planned on the anniversary to millions of Japanese viewers.

The video used simple black silhouettes of human figures superimposed over scenery filmed on Kauai to simulate the events on Niihau. The following is the English translation of the audio, presented here for the first time. Irene describes several interesting aspects never before mentioned. All of the original audio was in Japanese.

---

15   For That One Day; The memoirs of Mitsuo Fuchida, Commander of the attack on
      Pearl Harbor Mitsuo Fuchida, translated by D. Shinsato and Tadanori Urabe 2011,
      God's Samurai, Prange, Goldstein and Dillon, Brassey's Inc.
16   The Niihau Incident A. Beekman Heritage Press of Pacific

Irene Harada in "The Woman Who Was Called A Spy"

Interviewer question #1: " Did you actually see the airplane (*Zero*)?

Irene Harada: " Yes. (*Zero*) flew over a house we (*Irene and Yoshio*) lived. It made a full turn."

A narrator explains the beginning of the Niihau incident.

Irene Harada: " I am sorry for Mr. Nishikaichi. He just didn't want to die then. He said (to Irene and Yoshio) that he wanted to re-cover a paper (*a map*). Then Harada (*Yoshio*) decided to help him."

The narrator talks about the map Nishikaichi lost.

Irene Harada: "Mr. Nishikaichi desperately wanted to recover that map. Because Harada was a Japanese too, so he decided to help Nishikaichi. Harada knew that he would receive consequences for this act."

Interviewer question #2: "Was he fully aware of consequences?"

Irene Harada: "Yes. Once he decided to help (*Nishikaichi*). Although he (*Yoshio*) was the Hawaiian Nisei (*an American citizen born in the Territory of Hawaii from Japanese immigrant parents*), he still had a Japanese spirit."

Irene Harada: "It seems funny to recall this now. But he had this size knife (*indicating the size of knife with her hands*) with him (*for committing suicide*) when he left a house. I am sure that he prepared himself.

Interviewer question #3: "How did you feel when you were arrested for?

Irene Harada: "I was held at a prison on Kauai. I asked them if I looked a person who is capable to conduct any espionage activity. I told them that if I were smart enough to be a spy then I would have done something more extraordinary by that time. Since they kept telling me ridiculous false charges, I felt very resentful and talked back to them. I was very sorry for myself. I was alone in a small cell with a handcuff."

Interviewer question #4: "What about your children when you were arrested?"

Irene Harada: "Children could not come with me. I was by myself. They were brought to my sister's house."

Interviewer question #5: "Have you experienced being looked with disapproval because you were arrested for collaborating with a Japanese military?"

Irene Harada: "For a while after the incident, foreigners (*non-Japanese*) looked coldly on me. Just like they ostracized me. I asked a school to give my eldest son a special break, because even his teacher unfairly treated him in class. I was very sorry for him. Most people took good care of us. But some Japanese (*Japanese- Americans*) said, "'Harada did a stupid thing. He was a Japanese (*Japanese national, not Japanese-American*).'" I think I can't blame them for thinking in that way. Harada may have done a stupid thing one way or another. He knew that it (*helping Nishikaichi*) was not a task without a consequence when he decided to cooperate with him (*Nishikaichi*)."

Interviewer question #6: "How did you explain the Niihau incident to your children?"

Irene Harada: "I have not told anything to them. I thought that it just exposed the old wound. So I told them nothing. But they must have known. People must have told them."

Interviewer question #7: " You don't want to recall the incident even after 50 years?"

Irene Harada: "Sure, 50 years, isn't it? (*she does not elaborate*)

Five years later in 1996 Irene Harada died. She was 91 years old.

Aylmer Robinson had passed away almost thirty years earlier in 1967 at the age of 78. Ownership of Niihau transferred to Aylmer's brother, Lester, and his wife. After their deaths, the island's responsibility fell upon their boys, Keith and Bruce Robinson. Keith and Bruce grew up in close association with the Niihau Islanders, and had been tutored since birth on the religion, history, business and morals of their own family as well as the language, history and culture of the aboriginal community in their midst.

PART II

ON POINT

My wife Kathryn "KT" Budde-Jones and I were hired to help start the Pacific Aviation Museum (PAM) at Pearl Harbor, Hawaii in 2005. After learning about the project's existence, we had pulled no punches in trying to get involved. The museum was projected to be housed in the original bullet-scarred hangars on Ford Island attacked during the Japanese Pearl Harbor raid in 1941, near the *Arizona Memorial, Battleship Missouri* and the *USS Bowfin*.

The idea to start the museum had originally been that of Oahu resident John Sterling. Over time John had gradually gathered together a team of board members, largely comprised of retired military officers, to push the venture from daydream into reality. Years of effort had been invested to garner political traction, get site permission, and raise money. There now seemed enough momentum to carry the endeavor through.

Starting the museum was a leap of faith for everyone involved. KT and I quit our jobs in Florida, sold our house and bought one on Oahu sight unseen. We convinced a friend to put his restored WWII Stearman primary trainer on loan to the museum — the aircraft had actually been flown by George H.W. Bush when he was an aviation cadet in 1942. Another friend donated a rifle that had been recovered from the battleship *California* during its post-Pearl Harbor attack salvage. Others also felt compelled to donate artifacts on the basis of our involvement.

KT had been hired as the museum's Education Director, I was to be the Restoration Director. We both felt confident that our skill sets were up to the jobs, with educations, museum experience and years of prolific "warbird" (WWII-era military aircraft) restoration and flying experience. It also did not hurt to be well networked into the warbird community.

We arrived in Hawaii ready to go to work. Museum Director Allan Palmer had already hired his son Steven to produce graphics for the project. He had also employed Mike Wilson, an ex-subordinate from a prior museum as Curator, and later added "Mac" McKellar to construct exhibits. John Sterling's wife Kim was Allan's Administrative Assistant. We seven carried the responsibility of researching, developing, designing, and building every program and exhibit, while acquiring and restoring all artifacts and aircraft. There were already high expectations among the board members for the museum's anticipated "world–class" multi-million dollar first phase. The opening date for that phase had already been optimistically set for December 7, 2006.

Some serious problems threatened to stall our progress. Pearl Harbor is still an active Navy base as is Ford Island in its center. The old hangars on Ford Island that were to be leased to the museum were Navy property, and the final written agreement that would give us the property had been unexpectedly delayed for an unknown amount of time. The seed money committed to start the museum wouldn't be released until the museum had possession of the hangar property. The project's momentum was faltering in the bureaucratic log jam, with no clear indication which way the scales might tip. For the undetermined future, our "museum" offices were housed in a scruffy, mildewed old office block at the Honolulu airport.

KT was able to start developing some of her educational program concepts but I had little real work to do other than trying to acquire donations of equipment and building an architectural model of the first phase hangar to be used for planning displays. When not engaged in other activities, I had lots of time to explore ideas that could be developed into exhibits.

As a group, we all agreed that the theme of the first phase hangar of the museum should be centered on the aviation story of the Pearl Harbor attack and the events that followed immediately afterward. The rest of WWII, Korea, Vietnam and the Cold War would be covered in later phases. Since well over 1.5 million visitors a year already visited the nearby *Arizona Memorial* to learn about the Pearl Harbor attack, we all felt strongly that our own first phase should reflect the aviation component of that event.

A growing interest of mine was to try and find Japanese artifacts from the attack, something significant that would help the museum tell the story. Twenty-nine Japanese aircraft had been shot down that day, and many of the wrecks had been recovered. Pictures taken at the time showed significant and identifiable components at the crash sites. Finding anything recovered from one of those crashes now would be a real *coup* for the museum.

Over many years of visiting numerous other WWII-themed museums and interacting with WWII memorabilia collectors, I had only seen a few small scraps of metal that had been removed from those crashed aircraft by souvenir hunters. The airplanes, or major pieces of them just didn't seem to exist anymore. I began doing research, trying to find out what became of them.

Several months later I was ready to surrender my quest. From the limited information I had been able to find, it appeared that all the recovered wreckage had been brought to either the Navy or Army engineering hangars on Oahu for evaluation. Unique components were removed, disassembled and evaluated. Reports were written about the findings. After the engineers had removed what they wanted, and G.I. souvenir collectors had picked at the leftovers, the rest was scrapped.

Only one of the wrecks still eluded me. I knew a damaged Zero had crashed on the remote Hawaiian island of Niihau, and had a vague understanding of the rest of the story. A fragmentary old report indicated that the engine and propeller from the Niihau aircraft had been brought to Ford Island, presumably for investiga-

85

tion. There was no mention as to what happened to the rest of the airplane. It seemed highly unlikely that any of the Zero could still be out there, but I couldn't find any definitive indication that all of it had been removed.

To conclusively rule out the Zero's existence, I needed to talk to someone who had been to the privately owned island of Niihau. None of the locals I spoke with had ever been there, or even knew anyone who had. Engaging some of the museum's more well-connected board members to help me contact the owners of the island also failed. Niihau was living up to its name as "The Forbidden Island."

I was running out of ideas. I scanned the internet, trying different word combinations to conjure something new. In 2005, there was almost nothing referencing Niihau or any of its history beyond a brief mention on the *Pacific Wrecks* website and sites dedicated to Japanese airplane models. After hours of internet prospecting, I found an obscure reference to a convention of retired electrical engineers. The convention had occurred several years prior in Honolulu. One of the speakers at the convention had given a brief lecture about his recent trip to Niihau Island with a film crew. His name was Allan Lloyd.

I contacted the organization that had held the convention, but they were no help. As far as I knew, Allan Lloyd could have come from anywhere in the world to a convention in Hawaii. I wasn't even sure if he was American.

In the final stages of desperation, I looked up the name Allan Lloyd in an Oahu phone book, found a possible listing and dialed the number. No one picked up, but an answering machine requested I leave a message. I did. No return call. One week later I left another message. Again, no return call.

Another week passed. One morning I got a call from a woman. She was Allan Lloyd's daughter, while checking on his house she had heard my phone message. He was on a cruise. Yes, he was a retired electrical engineer. She would have him call me when he returned.

Days passed before I got the anticipated call from Allan. I got right to the point...

"Allan, did you give a talk about a visit to Niihau several years ago for a retiree conference here in Honolulu?"

"Yes. I heard a film crew had gotten permission to go out to the island and I talked myself onto the crew as a "gofer" so I could join them. I've been to all the other Hawaiian islands except Niihau, so I really wanted to go there and complete the list."

"Did you get a chance to see much of the island?"

" Yes, we saw quite a bit of it."

" By any chance did you see any old airplane wreckage out there?"

"The Zero? I took pictures of what's left of it."

" Wow, great - I'd love to see them. Did you meet Niihau's owner?"

" Yes, I know Keith."

"Do you have any contact information for him? I'd really like to talk to him."

"Yes, I have his number."

Allan wouldn't give me Keith's private number over the phone, but was interested in learning more about our museum project and my intentions for the Zero. He suggested we meet over lunch.

KT and I met Allan Lloyd as he suggested. Lloyd was an amateur WWII historian with a specific passion for the Battle of Midway. Before he would discuss anything about Niihau, we had to prove ourselves worthy. He first tested us, questioning our knowledge about events in WWII. After we satisfied him with our answers and the conceptual description of the museum, he began to open up about his experience on Niihau. Lloyd showed us pictures he had taken of the island including a couple he had taken of the Zero wreckage. The photos were a little disappointing, they only showed a few barely visible small pieces of twisted metal protruding out of dense, high weeds. It wasn't much, but Lloyd remarked that he hadn't examined the remains closely.

Lloyd very enthusiastically described an old Cletrac tractor he had seen during his Niihau visit. He briefly explained that it had been used to plow up the island before WWII to prevent Japanese aircraft from landing there. I hadn't heard this facet of the Niihau story before, obviously further study on my part was required. I was still primarily focused on the Zero, hoping an arrangement could be made so the museum could display the remains of this unique artifact for the public to see. Lloyd said that he would contact Keith Robinson, and would try to set up a meeting so we could discuss our interests with him in person.

I reported my success to our Director, Allan Palmer. We discussed not only the potential of an exhibit based on the artifacts, but that anything remaining of the Zero had a potentially important archaeological perspective- something that both KT and I had strong backgrounds in. If the museum didn't capture that aspect of the story as well, it would miss an important one-of a-kind opportunity in the eyes of historians and academia.

True to his word, Allan Lloyd called me several weeks later to report that Keith had agreed to see us. As soon as the arrangements could be made, Lloyd accompanied museum Director Allan Palmer and myself to Kauai to discuss our interests with Keith. Our meeting was set up in the back dining room of a small restaurant in Waimea.

Keith arrived as promised. He was dressed in working man's attire, sporting a green hard hat, which added a curiously disarming visual effect. He was courteous but initially understated during our presentation.

We explained the museum's optimum Pearl Harbor location, and the anticipated high number of visitors. Unique and compelling exhibits about the Pearl Harbor attack were needed, and the story of the Niihau Zero was a perfect fit. We hoped that he would consider loaning any Zero artifacts to *PAM* so we could build an exhibit around it.

Keith brought up the subject of the Cletrac and his uncle Aylmer's preparation of the island for the Japanese attack. After listening to his description of the activity, it was apparent that any story the museum presented about the Niihau Zero needed to include Aylmer Robinson's plowing up the island in anticipation of the raid. The Niihau story was getting a lot more interesting.

After we made our case, Keith said that he would discuss our meeting with his brother Bruce. The two of them would decide if they were interested in loaning artifacts to the museum. He cautioned us that he was already very unhappy about past representations of the events on Niihau, being particularly critical of Allan Beekman's "*The Niihau Incident.*" "Beekman never talked to any of the Robinsons, or the Niihau people," Keith said. "He was never on the island. I'm not sure where he got his information from, but his book is filled with inaccuracies. If we were to loan the relics to the museum, you would have to agree that I would be allowed to help with the way the story is presented to make sure it was told correctly." We assured him that his input would be crucial to the display.

Keith suggested that in the meantime, we might want to visit Niihau to see what remained of the Zero and the Cletrac. We would have to charter the Robinson's personal helicopter for the day to go out to the island, but Keith offered to accompany us as our guide. It was an extraordinarily exciting offer, and we returned to Oahu knowing that we were being granted entrance through a rarely opened door. Our trip to Niihau was scheduled in a couple weeks.

We still had little insight as to what actually remained of the Zero, or in what condition it existed. My own presumption was that the aircraft was still at the original crash site, but that was just a guess. There were so many questions to answer, and it required an organized approach. I wrote an archaeological guideline for a "pre-disturbance survey" (see appendix 2) for any artifacts found and the crash site area. Also listed were questions to be answered about the plowing and the Cletrac tractor as it related to the Japanese attack. I had found some copies of photos that Rev. Denise had taken of the burned out Zero before it was disassembled by the evaluation teams. Hopefully we would be able to compare the site features now to what it looked like then. I assembled some surveying gear, a metal detector, as well as video and still cameras for the trip.

On the big day our team flew back to Kauai and met Keith at the Port Allen airport. He was dressed as before and still sporting his green hard hat. The helicopter we would fly to Niihau in had been previously chartered from the Robinsons for use in the movie "*Jurassic Park*," some of which was filmed in Kauai. It was an ironic twist that we were now using it for our own visit to "The Forbidden Island."

We took off and headed out over the channel between Kauai and Niihau. The sea was quite rough with large whitecaps. As if reading my thoughts, Keith spoke over the intercom about the treacherous currents, huge waves and large sharks common here. I tried to imagine Hawila Kaleohano and the rest of the crew rowing across this broad strait of troubled water at night to alert Aylmer of the evolving danger on Niihau.

We approached the southern half of the island and Keith directed the pilot to orbit one of several dry lakes there. He pointed out ghostly but discernible furrows in the dried mud, laid out like a giant checkerboard. Here were the remainders of Aylmer's plowing project, their unlikely survival still confirming the long ago effort. The island was largely over grown now with "sour grass," as Keith called it, a type of plant that grazing animals wouldn't eat. The thick grass now hid most of the gradually eroding furrows from view. Apparently, seeds from bushes and trees eventually ended up in some of the furrows, the orientation of the now grown vegetation still copied the furrow's pattern in some areas.

We flew up the middle of the island to a landing spot near a small isolated shack adjacent to a rutted track that cut through a dried grass field. The helicopter dropped us off and quickly took off again to another location. Keith guided us to a spot near the track, and told us that the wreckage of the Zero had been collected and moved here from its prior resting place in the recent past. The original area was no longer appropriate, and the decision was made to move the remains before they disappeared.

The wreckage was hard to see in the tall grass. It was in sections and randomly scattered, but its presence was deeply moving. Arguably, this airplane had participated in the singular event that had drawn America into WWII — the most violent and transformative event in human history. It had also notably altered the history of this far-flung, otherwise unremarkable island. Even in its diminished condition it was by far the world's largest collection of artifacts from a Japanese aircraft shot down during the Pearl Harbor raid in the world.

The Zero's remains had been dumped here in an unorganized pile, some distance from where it originally landed. I had to quickly modify my "pre-disturbance" plan.

Since there was no important crash site data at this location, the scope of the wreckage could be recorded without further consideration. We pulled all the parts we could find out of the deep grass into the clear and I set up my camera gear to make a photo-mosaic of the artifacts.

The remains were largely skeletal, and most of the exterior surface paintwork had flaked or faded away exposing the still visible underlying red primer. Several pieces of the structure long shaded from the sun still showed some of the Zero's original exterior coloration, now faded to a light grey. There were even places where the unique, blue-green tinted lacquer painted on interior surfaces still glowed. Other surprising parts survived as well. Small wooden strips that had acted as chafe guards in the wing's aileron wells were still in place. There were original production markings that had been printed on the aluminum sheet metal at the time of its manufacture

Assembled photo mosaic taken of the Zero wreckage.

still faintly visible. The majority of the surviving structure seemed to be wing components, but in the rush to document the objects, it was hard to analyze the entire collection.

There were pieces that showed evidence of the fire when Nishikaichi and Harada torched the aircraft. I found the nose section of the centerline fuel drop-tank, flattened into a pie pan shape by high heat.

We had been joined by some Niihau islanders at Keith's request, who had arrived in an old surplus 4x4 roofless command truck for our transport around the island. Keith had told us we could take pictures of anything we wanted, but requested that we didn't photograph the islanders or their houses for privacy issues. I was too busy documenting the Zero to pay much attention, but it seemed that we were the object of interest to a growing number of the local men. The islanders had complexions derived from long hours in the sun, and some had strong Polynesian facial features distantly reminiscent of Easter Island statues. Their friendly and helpful nature manifested itself when one of them presented us with a previously unseen piece — a crankcase/blower section from a radial aircraft engine.

Keith talked to the fellow who had brought the piece in Hawaiian, the first time I had ever heard the language outside of a few commonly used words. They conversed briefly, and then switched to English for our benefit. Gilbert Kalaola Pahulehua Jr. (Niihau school principal in the 1950s-60s) told us that his dad had saved the engine part at his home over the years to keep it from being lost.

According to Gilbert, the engine case was from the Zero.

The part certainly had the patina of age, and there were old hacksaw marks where a couple of very small pieces had been cut off as if to sample the metallurgy. It had been separated from the engine by unbolting rather than by high speed impact. I had not previously studied Sakae 12 engine details, nor had anyone else in our party. We wanted to believe that it really was from Nishikaichi's plane, but remembered that Keith had told us of other old aircraft wrecks around the island. I also recalled the original report stating the Niihau Zero engine and propeller had been taken to Ford Island. The engine part was photographed from different angles, hoping that our continued research would confirm Gilbert's belief.

After we finished photographing the Zero wreckage, Keith had one of the islanders drive us to the crash site in the old 4x4. While en route, we talked to Keith about his own life on Niihau.

He had been born in the summer of 1941, ironically about the same time that Nishikaichi's Zero had been built in the Mitsubishi factory. As a little boy he used to play in the Zero's wreckage, pretending to be a fighter pilot. Keith and his brother had grown up amongst the islanders, and had heard their descriptions of the Nishikaichi/Harada event first hand. Like his uncle Aylmer, Keith had gotten a university degree on the mainland, and had never married. He had a passionate interest in preserving endangered endemic Hawaiian plants and the Monk seal population.

Keith mentioned that for many years during Aylmer's tenure, the ranch with its associated honey and charcoal business often struggled to produce enough income to support itself and the employment of the Niihau people. To cover expenses Aylmer sometimes sold up to $14,000 a month in personal stock to help sustain the endeavor and his employees. In the late nineties the Robinsons made the inevitable decision to reduce some ranch operations that simply weren't economically viable anymore. The family told the remaining islanders that they were welcome to stay in their houses and live on Niihau as long as they wished, but there would be fewer opportunities for employment. Those that wanted to could move to Kauai and work for the Robinson business on that island. Over fifty Hawaiians currently still called Niihau home.

We arrived at a spot near where the Zero had crashed on the very outskirts of Puuwai village. I had expected to see rows of mono-chrome plantation type housing as I had seen on Oahu, but here the colorful houses were scattered, looking as if their placement was based more on the preferences of the occupants rather than a master plan. As Keith led us on foot to the crash site, I could pick out famil-iar features portrayed in Rev. Denise's 1941 photographs.

The spot in the fence line where Nishikaichi crashed through.

The original fence line that Nishikaichi's plane had crashed through was still there, supported by iron-like kiawe fence posts. I had assumed that it had been a barbed wire fence but Keith correct-ed me, stating that all fences on the island had always been smooth wire, since animals can get badly injured on the barbs. He also told us that although fence posts were replaced over time as necessary, the physical location of the fence was the same as it had been during the time of the crash. I had brought copies of some of Denise's photos with me, hoping to correlate some of the large and uniquely shaped volcanic boulders visible in the 1941 crash site pictures with what we hoped to see today. Keith pointed out a nearby house that had been built close to where Hawila Kaneohano's burned-down dwelling had once stood. Unfortunately for my purposes, most of the exposed boulders including the ones from the crash site had been gathered up to build a low stone wall around the perimeter of the house's yard

The location where the Zero had come to rest next to the fence had been a dusty stock path in 1941. It looked much the same now, but the surrounding landscape was much more overgrown with tall grasses, bushes and trees than when Nishikaichi made his final landing. The large grazing animal population during Aylmer's time had done an effective job of keeping the island vegetation closely cropped. After a great deal of effort, I was able to locate two now dead but still identifiable trees and background topography matching the Denise photos. Using the fence line and the other corresponding features gave me enough information to accurately fix where the aircraft had come to rest.

By now our party had been joined by more islanders. I watched Keith interacting with them and listened to the still unfamiliar sound of the Hawaiian language when they spoke to each other. Even from our limited conversations with Keith, it was already apparent that he had been raised by a generation still valuing the continuation of their strongly held family's moral and belief system. That made Keith our closest touchstone to understanding Aylmer.

I noticed an interesting trait in Keith's personality. When we asked him if he knew of the direction Nishikaichi had been flying prior to the crash, he gestured while answering definitively, as if repeating a long held and repeated truth. Then he summoned several islanders in Hawaiian and discussed it with them, before confirming with us in English that they also concurred. In most cases during the rest of the day, Keith would directly reply to our questions with his understanding of the event or place, and then discuss his answer with an appropriate islander to corroborate his answer. Sometimes they added details he hadn't mentioned. It would have been easy for us to take him solely at his word if the islanders hadn't been present, but he preferred to add a final layer of accuracy by including the perspective of the Niihau people.

We took lots of photos of the crash site and surrounding areas, I also took numerous measurements and readings from several features to aid in a future analysis of the site. Keith then told us about the original Army evaluation team's concerns over the wreck's open and exposed position. Since there was expectation that the Japanese forces might return, they decided to quickly conceal the wreckage. The dismembered airplane was dragged back down the slope it had flown over during its final approach, and hidden amongst a small group of trees. The Zero's remains lay there for decades; it was here that Keith played in the wreckage as a boy. We drove about 200 yards down the slope to visit the spot.

Keith wasn't sure if all of the Zero artifacts had been moved to their current location and was agreeable to me trying our metal detector to locate anything that might remain. After some experimentation among the thick overgrowth, it became apparent that a major archaeological survey would be required to find any pieces of the Zero still here. With time running out, we moved on.

We passed by the old honey warehouse where Harada had hidden Aylmer's shotgun, and later joined with Nishikaichi to overpower the guard. There were actually two frame buildings standing next to each other, both long unused and in an advancing state of decay. It was from these humble structures that the insurgency against the people of Niihau had begun.

Our next stop was at the remains of the old Cletrac tractor. It was quite badly rusted and hadn't seen use since the early 1960s. Next to a nearby shed, and almost invisible in the dried undergrowth, were the two plows that had been used by the draft animals and the Cletrac to furrow the island.

Bruce (left) and Keith Robinson, owners of Niihau, stand next to the Cletrac trac-tor. The honey warehouse is partly visible in the upper-right background.

Niihau had never been tilled for large scale agriculture, the plow's only purpose was to prevent Japanese planes from using on the is-land. Standing next to the plows and the Cletrac while visualizing the cross-hatched furrows we had seen in the dry lake bed hours before really defined what had happened here. For over seven years, this privately owned island was prepared for the Pearl Harbor attack by private citizens at their own expense, all based on nothing more than a compelling prediction. The Niihau story was more important than Nishikaichi and Harada, or even the shot down Zero. Adding the account of the island's pre-attack preparation gave the museum a once-in-a-lifetime opportunity to present a truly unique story with powerful local ties to large numbers of visitors. Hopefully the Robinsons would grant us permission.

Keith was very familiar with the Billy Mitchell predictions about Niihau from discussions with his family as well as from his own research.

He also recalled his father and uncle Aylmer mentioning a "Major Jerry Brant" as the person who had told Aylmer about Mitchell's prophecy, and had convinced him to plow up the island. Keith hadn't been able to confirm the existence of any "Major Brant" outside of his family's oral history and was hoping to find additional proof that this person actually existed. I promised him that I would personally try to research Brant with the resources I had at my disposal.

We asked if there were furrows that we could inspect up close, and Keith suggested that we drive to one of the dry lakes as they were easier to view there. We bounced along a dry rutted path in the old 4 x 4, going just fast enough to avoid the cascade of red dust we towed in our wake. Keith mentioned that the area we were driving through was originally furrowed as well, but erosion and advancing sour grass made them hard to see.

The driver stopped short of the dry lake, and before the trailing dust cloud crested over us we hopped out of the truck to see what we could find. Sure enough, emerging out of the foliage near the edge of the lake bed were the weathered furrows, extending out across the dried mud like a giant tic-tac-toe game. As Keith had previously described, they were about 18 inches wide forming 100 foot squares. We took photos and measurements while trying to imagine the scale of doing this across the entire island. The furrows now were barely inches deep in their center, but originally had been deep enough to snag landing gear and flip an airplane on its back. Crude, but effective.

Up until now we hadn't seen much of Niihau's ranching legacy but as we progressed cross country near the dry lakes the island smelled strongly of barnyard. Remnants of the ranch stock population still wandered here. Tinder dry grasses, dusty dirt roads, abandoned old surplus trucks, pieces of rusty construction equipment, and the stockyard smell recalled sheep stations of central Australia or Texas cattle ranches, not Hawaii.

After we had finished exploring the sites specific to our visit, Keith took us to the northern end of the island. The roads were still just bumpy dirt tracks that shuffled through the scrub. As we followed parallel to the western shoreline, Keith described a Catalina PBY (a

Above: The remains of the furrows on one of the dry lakes.

Below: Shells are harvested from these beaches for beautiful Niihau shell necklaces. The reported PBY crash happened just offshore of this beach.

long range, amphibious search and rescue flying boat) crash that had happened just offshore as the first investigation team arrived on Dec. 16, 1941. Although he didn't know the exact reason for the crash, the Niihau islanders who had seen the airplane go down reported that it appeared to be in combat with a submarine. Keith respected the islander's observation skills, and wanted to know if I had any information about the event. I didn't, but I told him that I would look into it.

We stopped our journey north in sight of Puukole Point on the northernmost tip of the island. From here we could see Lehua Island, an old volcano cone, just offshore. We all got out of the truck to survey the beach; wide, pristine and devoid of people. We were on the opposite side of the island from Kii Landing where Hawila Kaleohano joined the others in the whale boat for their desperate passage to Kauai.

Unfortunately, as on all shorelines these days, there was a surprising amount of man-made detritus thrown up to and well beyond the dune line. Keith told us that the trash had been deposited by huge waves that often pounded the island in the winter. He added that there were no docks or piers on the island for boats to tie up because they were always quickly destroyed.

Our day on Niihau finished as we waited for the helicopter to come pick us up. The others in my party wandered nearby, killing time. Keith was standing by himself and I walked over to chat with him. Our conversation drifted into a discussion about a favorite subject of mine, WWII history. Keith's knowledge of the subject was a revelation. He had obviously spent a great deal of time at some point in his life researching and digesting the complicated evolution of the conflict. He was especially astute and accurate with many of the details that a casual student of history would rarely learn and never remember.

After the helicopter deposited us back on Kauai, Allan Palmer told Keith he would send him a copy of a loan agreement for he and Bruce to review while considering the decision of loaning the artifacts to the museum. All of our staff were even more excited about telling the Niihau story after seeing the island and the artifacts first hand. We thanked Keith for his hospitality and headed back to Oahu.

Back in our temporary offices, I began searching for information on Gerald Brant. If we could independently establish Brant's existence during that timeline, it would help confirm that aspect of Keith's family history.

My research struck gold quickly. In short order I was able to find that a Major Gerald Brant had testified on behalf of Billy Mitchell at Mitchell's court-martial, and had been posted in Hawaii in 1933, the same time frame that the Robinson family history stated his meeting with Aylmer had occurred. Keith had given us his private phone number, so I anxiously gave him a call. He was thrilled to hear that my research on Brant dove-tailed so well with his family's version of the event. After my conversation with Keith, I emailed Judith Bowman, Curator of the U.S. Army Museum of Hawaii at Ft. DeRussy, Honolulu. Judith had been very helpful on some previous research I had done, and I wanted to let her know about the furrows I had seen on Niihau and their connection to Billy Mitchell. No one I knew (outside Niihau) had ever heard of this story, and I was sure that other historians would find the discovery a rare and valuable treasure.

Judith wrote back:

"Furrows were built on the island of Niihau at the request of Major Gerald C. Brant, AC, Hawaiian Dept. probably in 1933. Between 1933 and 1941 the furrows were made at the expense of Niihau owners, Robinson family. This request originated from Billy Mitchell's theory that the Japanese will invade Pearl Harbor by taking over Niihau first as a staging area for aircraft. Find Mitchell's theory on strategic Bombardment concept. He wrote numerous articles for Hearst Publications, Liberty, Colliers, The Saturday Evening Post, and Outlook."

She finished her email with more time-and-place details about both Brant and Mitchell along with other references. Judith was already well versed on the subject. Her reply did add further confirmation to the story as Keith and I understood it.

Mike Wilson located a good quality photo of a Sakae 12,

the same engine that powered Nishikaichi's Zero. The picture showed important details of the engine case, allowing a comparison with the pictures I had taken of Gilbert's engine case on Niihau. It was a perfect match. Gilbert was right — his father, Kalaola, had saved part of the Zero.

With no other engine parts in evidence on the island, the old report I had found stating that the propeller and engine from the Niihau Zero had been taken to Ford Island couldn't be completely discounted. Gilbert's casing proved that the engine had been disassembled on Niihau. Perhaps what the report should have said was that SOME of the engine had been taken to Ford Island.

I also found information on the early morning PBY flying boat patrol aircraft crash offshore of Niihau that Keith had described. That story proved to be true as well, but the reported explanation for the crash of the Kaneohe NAS-based aircraft was "wind shear," rather than a battle with a submarine. Ensign Thomas Hillis' crew flying another Kaneohe based PBY-5 spotted the downed plane (11-P-5) off Niihau at 0855 on December 16, 1941 [16]. The after-action notes stated that all the crew members of the crashed PBY survived except two.

Niihau resident Apelahama Nizo's account of the PBY crash gives more details. He said that the big flying boat went down close to shore in relatively shallow water, and for a time its submerged nose was pressed into the sea floor while the tail protruded above the surface. The nearest rescue boat the islanders had at hand was an old, traditional wooden canoe two miles away from the crash site. The little Cletrac was run at full throttle as it towed the canoe's trailer over the furrows and rough ground to the scene.

Some of the PBY's crew had managed to inflate the aircraft's life raft, but were so badly injured that they were unable to make it to shore. The Niihau islanders quickly launched their canoe and were able to rescue the survivors, giving them food and shelter until they were picked up by the second PBY the following day.

This event was little more than a week after Nishikaichi's crash, and the reality of America's new war with Japan had set in even on remote Niihau, The islanders believed that the flying boat had likely

---

16   VP -14, aircraft serial number 2415 After action report 12/16/41

been shot down by a nearby Japanese submarine. Despite fear that the sub they believed to be in the area could easily surface and machine gun them during the rescue, they didn't hesitate to paddle out to bring in the injured crew. It was a heroic act. (see appendix 3 for the Keith Robinson perspective on this event).

Numerous other squadron reports were found describing sightings and attacks on Japanese submarines in the waters around Niihau during the weeks following the Pearl Harbor raid. It is not known if these were legitimate targets or misidentified whales by trigger happy flight crews. The results of this research was shared with Keith during follow up conversations.

I wrote a six page report on the data we had collected from Niihau including a forensic analysis of the crash site (see appendix 4). Keith contacted Allan Palmer, saying that he and Bruce were favorably inclined to loan us the artifacts, but a few important details needed to be worked out with the museum. Allan had taken over as the sole museum contact with the Robinson's, negotiating final contractual agreements with them. I refocused my attention on other projects.

The activity level in our offices had suddenly begun to ramp up, the stalemate over the museum's hangar lease agreement with the Navy finally resolved itself, and the money spigot finally cracked open. We quickly needed to acquire more aircraft. The museum desperately wanted an intact Japanese aircraft of any type used in the Pearl Harbor attack, but there weren't many good options. A few airframes brought back for evaluation at the end of WWII had survived to end up in government museums and weren't available to us. Only one private museum in the U.S. owned a flyable, completely authentic Zero but it was not for sale. Just about every other option was little more than incomplete, badly corroded, battle damaged junk recovered from island jungles.

Fortuitously, a private collector in California recently decided to sell an A6M2 Zero. The airplane had originally been recovered from Ballale Island in the 1960s, had been taken to Canada, and was restored to flight worthy condition for the Confederate Air Force. After years of aerial displays and difficult maintenance, it was transferred to Camarillo, California for repairs. Serious structural issues were discovered and the airframe was drilled apart. Enthusiasm to finish the job didn't match the scope of the work needed. After years of languish, the project was put up for sale.

I was sent to Camarillo to inspect the Zero. It was in a partial state of assembly, which worked to my benefit, allowing easier access to inspect the airframe's structure. Apparent right away were the compromises made during the aircraft's restoration to get it back in the air. An American Pratt and Whitney R-1830 engine had been substituted for the original Nakijima Sakae 12. The two engines were of similar size, configuration and horse-power, and parts for the American engine were much easier to obtain than the now extinct Sakae. Much of the original sheet metal skin had been replaced, and during the process many of the inspection hatches and access panels had either been changed or omitted. The wing tips no longer folded as they once did to allow more efficient storage aboard aircraft carriers.

What this Zero did have was most of its original internal structure, canopy, cockpit features, landing gear and fuselage fairings. This was very unusual for a flying restoration of what had once been a badly damaged, ex-combat veteran. Layers of poor workmanship had compromised its continued flying career, but the museum wasn't necessarily looking for an airworthy example, just one that would present well and was within their budget.

Museum founder John Sterling had wanted to obtain a more accurately restored example, but the board voted to purchase the plane. Since our own restoration shop was yet to be outfitted with all the tools needed to take on the job, Carl Scholl and Tony Ritzman of *Aero Trader* were contracted to rivet the airframe back together. I would assemble and paint the aircraft upon its arrival in Hawaii.

Since the museum's new Zero was the same model that participated in the Pearl Harbor raid, the decision was made to paint it the way Nishikaichi's looked on its final flight. That way, an exhibit could still be done highlighting Niihau even if things didn't work out with the Robinsons. If Keith and Bruce went through with the loan of the Niihau artifacts, our intact Zero, and their wreckage would support each other, giving an interesting "before and after" aspect to the story.

The author directs restoration department volunteers in assembling the museum's Zero.

Painting the intact Zero seemed easy at first as we had collected surviving fragments of the Niihau Zero's light grey paint still speckled on the wreckage. Curator Mike Wilson's forte was building model aircraft and imbedded in this passion was an obsession in finding the correct original color codes. He mined the opinions of others on modeling websites, finally settling on the advice of professional Japanese researchers introduced to him through David Aiken. Their findings showed that the original Japanese paint used on the Zero was actually a shade of medium green, which faded very quickly towards grey. Mike found photographic evidence to support this, so all we had to do was figure out how much it would have faded in the six months between the Niihau aircraft's manufacture and the Pearl Harbor attack. He and I shuffled through color chips in his office, finally settling on a color halfway between the exact green that the researchers had found and the grey from the wreckage.

Activities amongst the museum staff accelerated at a frenetic pace over the next few months. We acquired more aircraft, designed exhibits to present them and oversaw the conversion of our first hangar from its prior use as a gym back into its new life as a legacy building housing our first phase displays.

The museum's Zero finally arrived at our Ford Island location from *Aero Trader*. By now we had a basic restoration shop set up in a second hangar, where I led a team of volunteers in assembling the fighter. We had already prepared several other notable aircraft, but the Zero was something special. All of my staff were eager to work on it.

During the reassembly process I was able to thoroughly study details of its manufacture. This would be critical in identifying the many fragments of the Niihau wreckage. We then spent weeks preparing the Zero for paint.

I spent many long days painting the airplane, but in its completed state Nishikaichi's Zero had come back to life. It's importance to the museum granted it placement as the first aircraft visitors would see when they entered the display gallery.

All of our exhibit concepts were coming together except the Niihau artifacts. For some reason there had been an unresolved disconnect between Keith and the museum, and no further progress had been made. I still felt some ownership of the project, and feared the opportunity to secure the artifacts might be fading. This was a little difficult because I didn't want to step on Allan Palmer's toes since it was his responsibility to finalize all loan agreements, but time was getting away from us. I decided to test the waters by calling Keith to tell him about the museum's Zero and its paint scheme, perhaps during our conversation I might learn what the difficulty was.

During my call, Keith was upfront about his withdrawal from loaning the museum his artifacts. He had decided the contract Allan had given him was too long, too generic and too lawyerly. After asking him what points he would like to see on the agreement, he listed specific items, stated in plain English. I wrote them down, promising to see what I could do.

I reported my conversation to Allan, who took Keith's list of requirements and rewrote a simplified contract out of them. Within days we had a signed agreement between both parties. The compelling story and artifacts of Niihau would be presented to the world in arguably the most appropriate place; the epicenter of the Pearl Harbor attack.

MOVING (TIME)

Based on the photo mosaic of the Zero wreckage, we built appropriately sized crates and skids to transport the artifacts, and then shipped them to Keith on Kauai. The Robinsons would deliver the boxes to Niihau aboard a landing craft. As before, the museum staff would be transported via the Robinson's helicopter to Niihau were we would inventory the artifacts as they were packed for their trip to Oahu.

The much anticipated day for the recovery finally arrived. Allan Palmer and I were joined this time by KT, Steven Palmer and an additional videographer to document our activities. Keith flew in the helicopter with us while his brother Bruce piloted the landing craft from Kauai to Niihau. The island had recently benefited from a rare rainy spell, and the plant life there now visually shouted every shade of green.

Once we were deposited near the site of the Zero's remains, the inventory began. Every item was individually photographed, given a tag number and a brief description noted. A number of the islanders arrived in trucks with the crates they had just off loaded from the landing craft. After the artifacts had been tallied, the islanders packed them in the boxes. We worked quickly, but the process still took several hours. KT pointed out several interesting features on some of the pieces we hadn't seen before, but since our data collec-

The Robinson landing craft "Moli" arrives on Niihau to transport the Zero and Cletrac.

tion lagged behind the packing process, we postponed a detailed examination until later.

Once all of the Zero's parts had been sealed in their crates, we moved over to the Cletrac's location at Kiekie. Using some of the construction equipment at hand, the Cletrac was gently lifted from its decades old resting spot onto the shipping skid we had built. Years of exposure had degraded the old machine so badly that it looked like it might fall apart during the lift. We were all relieved to have it sitting safely in one piece on its skid. The remains of the plows were loaded as well.

With everything loaded up on trucks for transport to the landing craft, the museum staff's primary work for the day was completed. To capture some final images, Keith led us back to several of the points of interest he had shown us before. We stopped again at the honey warehouse, this time walking carefully among the fallen pieces next to the derelict building. Keith summoned Gilbert Pahulehua

Above: Keith Robinson, the author, and KT Budde-Jones during the Zero inventory.

Below: Keith Robinson being interviewed as the Zero's shipping crates are loaded. Foreman Gilbert Pahulehua is on the far right.

The Cletrac being moved from its resting spot, just yards from the honey warehouse.

Jr. who was related to Hanaike Niheu, the guard that Harada and Nishikaichi had overpowered with Aylmer's stolen shotgun. Gilbert told us that the building covered in corrugated metal was the actual building where Harada had hid the shotgun, and then lured the guard inside so he and Nishikaichi could capture him. Once under their control, they moved Hanaike to an adjoining wooden building, and locked him inside. After they had left, Hanaike jumped out of a second story window and escaped to spread the alarm.

There are two roads between the Kiekie area and Puuwai village. After Hanaike escaped, he took the higher, inland one and was not seen again by Harada and Nishikaichi. They had taken the lower, more direct route back to Hawila Kaleohano's house and the nearby Zero. They were delayed by their encounter with Mrs. Niheu and her kids, but commandeered her cart and eventually put the Zero's dismounted machine guns on it. The details that Gilbert and Keith provided helped make the Mizuha report come alive.

When the landing craft returned to Kauai, the boxed Zero components, the Cletrac and plows were loaded into shipping containers for their voyage to Oahu. Our work to design, interpret and present an exhibit based on the artifacts and the information we had learned needed to kick into high gear.

A week later the shipping crates arrived at the museum's restoration hangar. Using masking tape, I laid out a grid of one foot by one foot squares on the concrete floor. This would give us a scale to lay out the Zero's parts in correct orientation so we could identify exactly how much of the plane still existed. Once the physical locations of all the pieces relative to each other were established, the same plan could be mirrored in the exhibit, enabling visitors to more easily understand what they were looking at.

Having the museum's intact Zero nearby was a huge help in "mapping" the pieces on my measurement grid. It also proved invaluable in identifying small, disembodied fragments that didn't seem to fit with any of the larger pieces. Putting the Niihau Zero

The two honey warehouse buildings; the one on the right is where Harada and Nishikaichi overcame the guard (Hanaike Niheu). The partially obscured one on the left is where Niheu was locked up and eventually escaped.

Laying out the parts of the Zero in their correct relationships.

Comparing parts of the Niihau Zero to the museum's Zero while the latter is being prepared for paint.

back together was never possible; it was a jigsaw puzzle with most of the pieces missing. The remains were more like a major dinosaur fossil discovery.

Once the Zero's extremities had been established on the grid, the size of the exhibit space needed for it, the Cletrac, and the plows to be staged together was calculated. Our intent for the display was to lay the wreckage out as if it had been left at the original crash site. Mike Wilson and Steve Palmer took on the task to finalize the development of the display's concept and story, integrating it into the rest of the museum's exhibits.

Historian David Aiken gave me some unexpected insight on the whereabouts of one of the major missing pieces of the Niihau airplane. The old report I had found stating that the propeller had been taken to Oahu turned out to be true. David's further research placed the prop's current location with a private aviation club on the island. I knew some of the "*Quiet Birdmen*" already; their clubhouse was literally next door to where our original temporary offices had been at the Honolulu airport. I notified Allan Palmer of this latest evolution, and a phone call later we were invited to visit the "QB" clubhouse during their next meeting.

Allan and I got our chance to visit the QB as promised. Sure enough, mounted on the wall of their clubhouse was a three bladed prop, about the right size as the one that would have been on Nishikaichi's airplane. Among the non-related photos and memorabilia surrounding the prop was a brief description of the Niihau Zero, including a statement that the propeller had been removed from it. The prop's appearance was different

The Niihau Zero prop in its current location.

now from the one detailed in Rev. Denise's photos. A conversation with one of the QB guys filled in the gaps.

The two bent blades had been hammered flat so it would be easier to hang on a wall. The prop had been sandblasted as well, all the original paint and markings had been removed. The hub counterweights were gone. Although it was satisfying to have located another important piece of the plane, it was sad to see that much of the original historical value of the piece had been lost during its "restoration."

The museum's Zero, in Nishikaichi's markings, is pushed over to the display hangar.

Allan appealed to the QB members to donate or loan the prop to the museum so it could be displayed to the public with the rest of the Niihau artifacts. They voted on it, and in the end decided to keep it in their private club. I was disappointed by their decision, but with the museum's drop-dead opening date looming, we had other important things to fret over.

My restoration team and I were really pushing hard to complete all of the aircraft in time for our compressed schedule. The design of the first phase exhibits required that each aircraft had to be put in place before its individual display's construction could be finished. This had to happen in the correct sequence to allow the correct assembly of the other exhibits. Some of the aircraft were suspended from the ceiling, others were on diorama stages or the floor. We towed, pushed and lifted them into place among the many dozens of workers still laboring on the unfinished display spaces and general construction.

It was a special moment when the museum's Zero was brought over from the restoration hangar. Nishikaichi's markings which looked so bright and fresh on it in the Pearl Harbor sunshine would be a real visual counterpoint to the broken and forlorn

The Niihau Zero being laid out on its grid prior to the display's completion.

remains of the actual Niihau Zero. The comparison for the visitors would be dramatic.

Once the airplanes had all been located in the display gallery, we brought the large pieces of the Niihau Zero over to do a final layout check on their display diorama. Marker wires were attached to a metal grid that would be covered by the faux "Niihau soil" of the finished exhibit. The marker wires would protrude through the soil, allowing attachment points for the artifacts.

Photos taken of the crash site were now a bigger-than-life panoramic wall across the back of the exhibit. Replica soil, rocks and grasses in the foreground would be blended into background graphics, hopefully giving visitors a sense of the place. A railing to keep people away from the artifacts had yet to be fabricated, I suggested getting some kiawe posts as used on the real fence line. Dedicated volunteer Arnold Kanehiro quickly found the perfect cuttings and we mounted them across the front of the display, strung with some rusty looking movie-prop rubber barbed wire left over from another exhibit. It looked right, and the fake barbed wire kept the visitors at a respectful distance.

The Niihau display placed the Zero wreckage on the left of the wreck site diorama, and the Cletrac, along with the plows were on the right, next to a shed like the one it had been parked next to on the island. A story board in front of the wreckage described the Niihau event, and one near the Cletrac told of Mitchell's and Brant's influence on Aylmer, convincing him to plow up the island in preparation for an attack on Pearl Harbor. A continuous loop video additionally supported the storyboards.

The museum's Zero was staged as if on the *Hiryu's* flight deck; the background was a dramatic sunrise. The actual Niihau Zero display was hidden from the viewing area of the Zero. Visitors wouldn't normally see it until exploring other displays on the Pearl Harbor attack.

The first phase of the museum opened on time to rave reviews, with visitors especially fascinated by the Niihau story and exhibit. Aylmer's preparation for the Pearl Harbor attack, Nishikaichi's crash, and the Niihau islanders' handling of the ensuing events highlighted a largely unknown but important part of Pearl Harbor history, all with strongly local DNA. The Cletrac, plows, and the actual Niihau Zero added an irreplaceable presence of authenticity to the story. However, as compelling as the exhibit was, all was not right.

Unfortunately, neither Keith nor Bruce Robinson had been consulted during the hurried scripting of the exhibit storyboards and video as we had promised. This omission caused real heartburn between the Robinsons and the museum, at a time when the museum itself was undergoing critical personnel changes. Director Alan Palmer and graphic artist Steven Palmer both left to pursue other projects. Curator Mike Wilson soon departed as well. Freshly hired interim Director Richard Beckerman appointed me interim Curator in addition to my normal restoration duties. Now with a laundry list of changes, improvements, and new exhibits to design and implement, my first task was to try and mend fences with the Robinsons. Fortunately, Keith was agreeable to my overtures and he shared his insights as I worked through a rewrite of the exhibit's signage. During the process, none of the presented facts actually changed, but the experience helped to convince him that we valued both the Robinson's and the Niihau people's perspective in telling the story. The exhibit's necessarily compressed version of the Niihau story was

Above and Below: The Niihau Zero/Cletrac display at the Pacific Aviation Museum.

Visitors see the recreated Nishikaichi Zero before viewing the actual Niihau Zero.

still told on two story boards and a video presentation, with additional details from trained docents who guided the visitors through the display gallery.

The hard work and long hours the museum staff continued to pour into the fledgling operation began to pay dividends. New exhibits came on line as fast as Mac MacKellar and I could research, design and build them. Attendance numbers grew to meet our expectations, and the visitors were enthusiastic about their museum experience. Aside from the numbing work schedule, we were all proud of our "baby."

Notification of an upcoming lecture by Allan Beekman's daughter about his book "*The Niihau Incident*" passed through the museum staff. The evening presentation was to be at the Aiea Library, just down the hill from our home. I was busy that evening doing research for a future exhibit, but my wife, KT, was joined by a number of museum volunteers, curious to hear what would be discussed.

KT would be the only person at the lecture that had actually been to Niihau, talked to the islanders or the Robinsons.

After the lecture finished there was a question and answer session. A diminutive, older Japanese-American woman spoke up about her own personal interpretation of the events on Niihau. She stated that Yoshio and Irene were innocent of any collaboration with the aviator when he attempted to take over the island and threaten its people, that the Haradas were simply full of traditional Hawaiian "Aloha spirit", and had only wanted Nishikaichi to feel welcome and at ease. From her perspective, their actions had been completely misunderstood.

This statement brought smiles and a few chuckles, particularly among the museum staffers. Her theory seemed slightly pathetic, particularly against the mountain of research we had amassed on the subject. No one took her seriously.

We should have.

PART III

PERSPECTIVES

A common catch-word among museums today is "re-interpretation." Strictly speaking, it refers to adjusting a long-held understanding of an event due to new evidence, facts or documentation. A well known example of the re-interpretation concept concerns the European discovery of the New World. For centuries, Christopher Columbus' expeditions of discovery were given credit as the first Western presence in the Americas. In recent decades, a growing number of archeological finds have made a strong case that Norsemen may have preceded Columbus to the New World by centuries.

Legitimate historians will doggedly compile every piece of data they can about an event, to identify the most accurate flow of history. If additional new facts become available, they will adjust their conclusions as necessary to maintain an accurate heading on the compass of truth. Although World War II was captured as never before in history by photographs, films, official reports, magazines and newspapers, there are still surprising events being unearthed by diligent researchers. Historian Ron Drez wrote of an unexplained hitch in the crucial timeline of the Nazi initial advance during the Battle of the Bulge. The mystery was resolved decades later by John Eisenhower's investigation into a previously unknown stand of eighteen determined American sharpshooters who pitted themselves effectively against the might of the massed German juggernaut at tiny Lanzerath, Belgium. Their action in part now explains why the Nazi's time-critical advance did not proceed at the needed pace to achieve their goals [17].

As has been the case throughout human history, WWII and its participants will fade further into the past, and subsequent generations will re-interpret those events within the context of their own experience and education, sometimes tinted with contemporary personal, political or cultural biases.

In the mid 1990s, *The Smithsonian Air and Space Museum* became the center of a major controversy, suffering a self-inflicted black eye over its proposed B-29 *"Enola Gay"* exhibit. The *Enola Gay* was the actual bomber that dropped the atomic bomb *"Little Boy"* on Hiroshima, Japan on August 6, 1945. Rather than just display the aircraft and describe the mission facts as documented, the museum decided to use a modern interpretive presentation that did not mesh with widely held beliefs about the event. The controversy shows how sensitive issues involving WWII can become.

One of the principal entities contesting the planned display was the Air Force Association, which later published a lengthy article by John Correll, detailing broad public and government angst over the *Smithsonian's* handling of the exhibit. The nature of the display's script had quickly riled *The Air Force Association*, *The American Legion*, other veteran's groups, surviving *Enola Gay* crew members, museum docents, and many thousands of museum magazine subscribers. To them, the proposed exhibit signage was grossly unbalanced, portraying the Japanese as victims rather than as the aggressors in WWII, while additionally theorizing that the atomic bomb should not have been dropped at all.

Public reaction to the proposed exhibit was so strong that the U.S. Senate held two public hearings over the matter. During testimony, *Smithsonian* Board of Regents member Rep. Sam Johnson (R Texas) stated that while the *Enola Gay* "was not the only exhibit that had been overcome by political correctness and revisionism, I do want to stress that the majority of exhibits at the *Smithsonian* are very

17   Twenty Five Yards of War by Ron Drez, Hyperion

impressive and historically accurate." Rep. Ike Skelton (D-Missouri) wrote *Air and Space* director Martin Harwin a letter on September 8, 1994, stating he was "outraged by the sympathetic manner in which Japanese Imperialism is portrayed in the *Enola Gay* exhibit" and that "it is a sad day when the *Smithsonian Institution* must be urged to accurately report American history."

On September 23, 1994, a Sense of Senate unanimous vote declared the script "revisionist and offensive." Adding further fuel to the fire, Rep. Sam Johnson (R-Texas) obtained minutes on December 19, 1994 from a May 1994 *Air and Space* staff meeting discussing the exhibit's script having been sent to city officials in Nagasaki and Hiroshima for their editorial comments - all in an effort to avoid offending them. The team that had developed the exhibit reportedly did not interview or consult with any U.S. veterans about their views of the subject.

A February 1995 editorial in *The Washington Post* provided a profound summation: "It is important to be clear about what happened at the *Smithsonian*. It is not, as some have it, that benighted advocates of a special-interest or right-wing point of view brought political power to bear to crush and distort the historical truth. Quite the contrary. Narrow-minded representatives of a special-interest and revisionist point of view attempted to use their inside track to appropriate and hollow out a historical event that large numbers of Americans alive at that time and engaged in the war had witnessed and understood in a very different - and authentic way [18]." With pressure now at the boiling point, the proposed exhibit was scrapped and Director Harwin was forced to resign. The *Enola Gay* was eventually displayed with basic signage about its mission, without any of the modern "re interpretation" of the event that had caused so much furor [19].

In 2008 The *Pacific Aviation Museum* at Pearl Harbor would also find itself in the cross hairs over one of its exhibits. In this case, the

---

18 The Smithsonian and the Enola Gay: a retrospective on the controversy 10 years later by John T. Correll April 2004 Accession # ADA466911 Air Force Association, Arlington, VA.

19 Sam Johnson and Senate Committee from Air Force Magazine July 1995 vol 78 no. 7 p.23

challenge came from a small but locally influential source. The *Pacific Aviation Museum*, as with other like institutions, derived a portion of its income from state and federal grants. This government money does not flow in perpetuity, so periodically the museum applied for additional funds. It was during one of these application cycles that the first challenge of an exhibit involving the Niihau events began.

On January 27, 2008, a letter was sent to Hawaiian State Senator Lorraine R. Inouye, Chair of Intergovernmental and Military Affairs. It was written by the very same woman who had publicly absolved the Haradas of any misdeeds during the *Niihau Incident* lecture in Aiea. She and her husband were not originally from Hawaii, they had been lawyers in Chicago. For the purposes of this story, we will refer to her as simply as "Mrs. X." Her letter follows:

I am (Mrs. X), a citizen of Hawaii. On January 11, 2008, my husband xxx and I visited the Pacific Air Museum. After watching a brief film we were ushered into the display area and to the left was the remains of the Zero, which crashed on Niihau. The picture of the pilot, Shigenori Nishikaichi, and the picture of one of his rescuers, Mr. Yoshio Harada, accompanies the display. The story written in large letters include these words:

    1) "Nishikaichi was **aided** by Mr. Harada..."
    2) "Yoshio Harada, a Japanese laborer who **conspired** with Nishikaichi to overthrow the island..."
    3) "...one of the aircraft's guns, which Nishikaichi **and Harada** used during **their** siege...

Their is also a handout titled Aviator's Flight Log Book which states (page 2) "the consequences of the events leading to his, (Nishikaichi's) death led to the eventual internment of Japanese-Americans in Hawaii and the West Coast of the United States." These are conjectures and unproven. The author of The Niihau Incident, Mr. Allan Beekman, admits that he could never get a

definitive answer from Mr. Harada's widow, Umeno
(Irene) Harada, about what was in her husband's
mind as far as motives for helping the pilot.
Professor Patsy Sumie Saiki, author of Gan-
bare, states the pilot spoke with them one evening thusly, "... I want to thank you for you
have been my friend, even though you know I'm the
enemy." Mr. Beekman and Prof. Saiki wrote their
stories after interviews with Mrs. Harada.

What are not conjectures and not unproven are
the report of the studies begun in 1982 by the
Congressional Commission which concluded that
the root causes of the Internment was "race
predudice, war hysteria, and a failure of political leadership" which led to the passage of the
Civil Liberties Act of 1988 which was signed by
Ronald Reagan. This resulted in the presidential
apology and $20,000 monetary redress payments to
the survivors of the Internment!

I am all for the granting of the one million dollars to the Pacific Aviation Museum but
only after the Museum leaders agree to a meeting
with the following willing persons:(she lists
the names of five people) to get the Niihau story
corrected.

Sincerely,
(Mrs. X)
(her address)

A copy of "Mrs. X's" letter was soon forwarded to *The Pacific
Aviation Museum* and was circulated among the senior staff. By this
point in time, many thousands of people had visited the museum,
and complaints about the exhibits, including the Niihau display, had
been negligible. "Mrs. X" had used an unusual tactic, challenging
the exhibit's content first by trying to influence the museum's financ-
es, rather than engaging in a direct conversation with the museum's
director or curatorial department about her concerns. A docent
who had given tours on the day "Mrs. X" visited the museum re-

ported that he remembered an older woman asking if the museum received government grants.

In her letter, "Mrs. X" labeled Yoshio Harada a "rescuer," and implied that Allan Beekman had not been able to draw any conclusions about the event due to his unproductive interviews with Irene (Umeno). "Mrs. X" did not mention Beekman's book had used terms such as "conspirators" and "insurgency" to describe the Nishikaichi/ Harada relationship, while defining Yoshio (and to a lesser degree Irene) as partners with Nishikaichi in the ensuing threats and violence against the Niihau islanders. After interviewing Irene, Beekman had written that in his judgement she had "bet on the wrong horse," and had spent the rest of her years bitter about it [20].

"Mrs. X" was clearly trying to make an association between declarations within in the Civil Liberties Act of 1988 (see appendix 5) and her complaint about the Niihau exhibit, but a direct connection was elusive to the staff at first reading.

Certainly, one part of her protest did have merit. The "Aviator's Flight Log Book" booklet she mentioned had been produced as a free souvenir for the museum visitors. The connection between the Niihau Harada/Nishikaichi story and the internment/relocation issue, however speculative, had a stubborn history. The booklet had been conceived early in the museum's genesis, and its author(s) had improperly added the incorrect extrapolation. *PAM's* displays were centered on military aviation events surrounding Pearl Harbor and the rest of the Pacific: it had no plans to explore the subject of internment/relocation in any of its current or future exhibits. Somehow, the unsubstantiated statement in the handout had gotten past the review process, and the inaccuracy was immediately excised from existing and future copies the booklet.

By now the museum had gained a vibrant volunteer staff of several hundred individuals who assisted the employees in running the operation. A large percentage of these people were Japanese-American, many of whom were some of the most enthusiastic and dedicated of all. None of them, nor the numerous Japanese-Americans visitors who had already toured the museum had ever questioned the au-

---

20   The Niihau Incident, A. Beekman, Heritage Press of Pacific

thenticity or appropriateness of the Niihau exhibit. Still, "Mrs. X's" protest warranted further investigation.

As Director Ken DeHoff began to explore "Mrs. X's" concerns, he found that she had assembled a team of lawyers and a sympathetic local university professor to challenge the exhibit. Her first desire expressed to DeHoff was to have several words that linked Harada to Nihsikaichi's aggressions struck from the exhibit signage, but her lawyers mentioned that they wanted the exhibit permanently removed.

Key staff members of all the Pearl Harbor historic attractions (the *Arizona Memorial*, the *USS Missouri*, the *USS Bowfin*, and the *Pacific Aviation Museum*) regularly interacted with each other over education programs, marketing and other shared interests. Word spread quickly through the other organizations about the Niihau exhibit challenge. We soon learned that "Mrs. X" had previously protested parts of the *Arizona Memorial's* presentation.

Before being ferried out to the *Battleship Arizona's* resting place, *Arizona Memorial* visitors watch an introductory film about the Pearl Harbor attack. "Mrs. X" had objected to several parts of the film and successfully induced the National Park Service (which manage the *Arizona Memorial*) to edit out the parts of the film that were in conflict with her interpretation of the *Civil Liberties Act of 1988*.

The introductory film had originally mentioned Army Lt. General Walter Short's decision to park the Army's planes close together and in the open at Hickam and Wheeler Fields where they could easily be watched for sabotage, rather than being scattered around the field or out of view in protective revetments. As war with Japan began to look more inevitable, Short considered the substantial resident population of both Japanese nationals and Japanese-Americans on Oahu and decided to issue the order [21]. Unfortunately, the grouped planes made convenient targets for the Imperial Japanese Navy pilots and many were destroyed. This order and its effects have been well documented in numerous books and studies on the subject.

---

21   A Naval Intelligence report dated Dec. 4, 1941 stated "Out of a total population of 423,330 in the Hawaiian Islands, there are 157,905 Japanese, approximately one third of which are aliens."

"Mrs. X" found this subject contrary to the Civil Liberties Act of 1988, a document that states grave injustices were done to citizens and permanent residents of Japanese ancestry "...without any acts of espionage or sabotage documented by the Commission... [22] " Based on this, the mention of General Short's 1941 documented order to reduce the possibility of sabotage from any person of Japanese ancestry on Oahu was edited out.

Another problem in the introductory film cited by "Mrs. X" was the use of an original film clip shot immediately after the Pearl Harbor attack. The scene showed an unidentified field worker of apparent Asian descent going about their work in an Aiea cane field, seemingly oblivious to the burning ships of Battleship Row in the background. There was no indication as to the sex or nationality of the worker.

"Mrs. X" and her supporters had the National Park Service digitally remove the worker from the original film segment, presumably so viewers would not assume that people of Japanese descent on Hawaii were unsympathetic to the devastation of the attack [23].

The news of the alteration of the *Arizona Memorial's* introductory film was surprising on several levels, particularly that historically recognized and documented events captured both in writing and film had been deliberately erased as if they had never happened. The Niihau exhibit was now in the crosshairs. *PAM's* staff had gone to great lengths to assemble and corroborate as many facts as possible from the original reports, the Niihau islanders, the Robinsons, and the artifacts themselves to develop the exhibit, nowhere in the exhibit signage was there a mention of espionage or sabotage, key elements that "Mrs. X" often referred to from *The Civil Liberties Act of 1988.* Harada's actions could be seen as treason, a specific not mentioned in the *Act* [24]. The whole episode — like Niihau Island itself, refused to fit easily into a box.

Historian Daniel Martinez of the *Arizona Memorial* suggested a possible means for resolving the issue between "Mrs. X",

22   Commission on Wartime Relocation and Internment of Civilians
23   Source: Daniel Martinez, Historian, Arizona Memorial
24   The U.S. Constitution (Section 3) defines treason as "...levying war against (the United States), or adhering to their Enemies, giving them Aid and Comfort."

her supporters, and *PAM*. His idea was to form an independent review committee to evaluate the research used for the exhibit,the exhibit itself, and the contents of the signage. The committee would also consider "Mrs. X" and her supporter's arguments against the display. Both parties would have to agree to the judgement of the committee, no matter the outcome. The idea had great merit; with strong emotions present on both sides, an independent review committee could defuse any further escalation.

Before the committee idea was fully developed, a four-page "Open Letter to the Pacific Aviation Museum and its State, Federal and Private Sources of Funding" arrived on a *Japanese American Citizen's League of Hawaii* (JACL) letterhead. The letter described "grave concerns" about the Niihau exhibit and spent considerable space comparing the display to a book written by Michelle Malkin called *In Defense of Internment*. According to the letter, Malkin's book "describes the events of Niihau in an inflammatory way," and tried to make the case "... that the events on Niihau led to E.O. 9066" (Roosevelt's executive order that lead to the internment/relocation of people of Japanese ancestry on America's West Coast).

The letter also discussed a number of topics, including the successful campaign to seek redress, that no instance of sabotage or espionage by anyone of Japanese ancestry in Hawaii or elsewhere in America had been proven, and mentioned that patriotic Japanese-Americans had served in the 100th Battalion and 442nd Regimental Combat team, among others. It added "We regard the Niihau exhibit in the same light as the excised Pearl Harbor (*Arizona Memorial?*) film clip, and are prepared to oppose the continued existence of this exhibit with equal dedication."

Direct criticisms of the actual exhibit then followed. The letter complained that the exhibit was too large compared to other displays in the gallery. "It was not really about aviation at all, but an isolated incident having to do with a Japanese pilot and one person of Japanese ancestry." The Billy Mitchell prediction and the plowing of Niihau were "a ridiculous stringing together of curious trivia." "The storyboards reveal inflammatory and selective word choices... conspired, aided," etc. The final sentence in the letter finished with

"...we believe that the exhibit should be removed in its entirety and replaced with something more proportionally related to the history of aviation in the Pacific. [25]"

The Hawaiian *JACL* found the existence of the display "insidious" and "deeply damaging," but had not offered any contrary historical evidence to the Nishikaichi/Harada relationship the exhibit currently described. Clearly, any committee evaluating the positions of both sides would have its work cut out for it.

As negotiations began over establishing the independent review committee, several of us at *PAM* began additional research, casting a wider net for further confirmation of the facts as we knew them, or information that would prove us wrong. KT's long-held research skills proved particularly effective in finding primary source documents and reports, as did Gary Meyers efforts.

Personal accounts, period newspaper stories and official documents provided broader details, but nothing discounted our understanding of the event. Interestingly, the *Encyclopedia of Japanese American History,* produced by the *Japanese American National Museum,* was found to have mentioned the episode under the heading **"Niihau incident."** The encyclopedia's brief overview of the story was familiar, and said of the Nishikaichi/Harada relationship: "...As days went by, Harada and Nishikaichi talked and the latter became more and more agitated. He finally decided to go after his stuff; for whatever reason Harada decided to try and help him. Both men were armed..." The encyclopedia's final statement on the narrative reads: "This incident raises questions about possible Japanese American cooperation with the Japanese in the event of an invasion, though it provides little insight because of the unusual conditions on Niihau and the unclear reasons behind Harada's actions. [26]"

Discussions between key board members of the *Pacific Aviation Museum,* "Mrs. X," and her supporters led to the mutual acceptance of Daniel Martinez's independent review committee concept. "Mrs. X" and her supporters selected committee members

25　JACL of Hawaii letter March 18, 2008, Jones Collection
26　Encyclopedia of Japanese American History, Japanese American National Museum, Brian Niiya, Editor. Page 302

they wanted to represent their interests as did *PAM*. None of those chosen had been to Niihau, nor had they talked to the islanders or the Robinsons. After both sides agreed to the roster, the museum prepared a catalogue of the research used in the exhibit for the committee to examine. There would be no mention of Irene Harada's Japanese television interview in the reference materials, because it had not been used in any part of the exhibit.

Some weeks passed before the committee completed its task, and its verdict was a compromise, with no particular favor granted to either side. Committee members agreed that the museum's signage was consistent with events as reported by the Niihau islanders, interpreted by Aylmer Robinson and as documented by Lt. Jack Mizuha. Despite that, they expressed concern that the display might stir up old, unjust race relations issues that the Japanese-American community had spent years trying to dispel, and that words describing the Nishikaichi/Harada relationship such as "conspired" were overly provocative. There was a suggestion that Aylmer might have possibly "filtered" the story as he translated the islander's comments to Lt. Mizuha, (the review committee members were not aware that the islanders also spoke English) and that since many of the participants were now dead, there was no way to prove the account's accuracy.

The review committees recommended that the display should just state the appropriate aviation aspects of the story, and avoid Harada's disloyalty. Museum visitors who wanted more information on the subject should be directed to read books about it — a surprising suggestion since the most widely available book was Beekman's, which pulled no punches in incriminating the Haradas [27]. The review committee also did not comment on the Mitchell and Brant connection or Aylmer Robinson's plowing preparation for the Pearl Harbor attack as rebuffed in the *JACL* letter, nor the physical size of the exhibit.

The museum's board avoided continued threats over loss of funding and further conflict over the exhibit by agreeing to the review committee's recommendation. With the crisis seemingly resolved, the display remained intact, albeit with modified signage, and re-

27   The Niihau Incident, Alan Beekman, Heritage press of the Pacific

mained a popular component of the visitor experience. One major hurdle remained: the Robinsons. *PAM* needed to convince Keith and Bruce Robinson that it was still a good custodian of the story when the signage was changed.

Keith Robinson was consulted as the new signage was composed but he did not like the script's downplay of Yoshio Harada's involvement, feeling Harada's act of stealing Aylmer's shotgun was pivotal to understanding why the event spiraled beyond a simple enemy plane crash and a POW. He, his family, and the people of Niihau had all lived with the story their entire lives; to be told that this aspect could not be presented as it was understood and originally documented, was offensive to him. Keith personally saw the people of Niihau as heroes who had bravely dealt with the violence that Harada had caused when he joined with Nishikaichi against the islanders. The Robinsons refused to approve the replacement signage.

KT and I would eventually leave Hawaii and *PAM* permanently to deal with chronic aging-parent issues on the mainland. At this writing, the Niihau artifacts are still on display there, but with an uncertain future.

One unexpected and dramatic development came to light that no one had anticipated. Internet information on Niihau, which had been so sparse when I first searched for information on the subject, had exploded. Descriptions of the event, opinions, comments, and reference "hits" now gave pages of options when entering key words such as Niihau, Niihau Zero, Harada or Nishikaichi. Discussion of the subject had leapt past anyone's ability to control it.

LOOSE ENDS AND MAGIC

On July 23, 1948, Aylmer Robinson wrote a three page letter to Gwenfread Allen, who was a Research Associate in History for the Hawaii War Records Depository. Ms. Allen had previously submitted her understanding of the Niihau story to Aylmer, and his letter to her was sent in response to clarify several points of her narrative. Comments in his reply about the plowing and the reason for Nishikaichi's landing on Niihau add some additional intriguing possibilities.

Aylmer wrote: "At Army request Niihau Ranch had previously furrowed all areas where it was thought planes might land..." This suggests, but does not prove, that Brant may have implied to Aylmer that their meeting was of a more official nature than has been understood. Did Brant just let his uniform do the talking, or had he been directed to approach Aylmer about Mitchell's prediction by a superior? Unfortunately, as of this writing, no known documents support the latter, and Brant's personal papers are currently in the possession of a descendant who has so far not made them public.

Aylmer offered other insights in his letter: "I believe the statement that the Japanese pilot announced he was taking the island for Japan is not correct. I acted as interpreter for the Army in getting its record on December 14, and have discussed the whole episode with the Niihau people who figured in the affair many times, but have never heard that claim from any of them. By what I heard the pilot was at first reticent, but later admitted to having bombed Honolulu and Pearl Harbor *(referring to the primary target of the raid rather than Nishikaichi's portion of it?)* and stated he was trying to locate the carrier but had failed to do so. [28]"

If Aylmer's understanding about Nishikaichi not being able to find his carrier is accurate, that would help to clarify why the aviator finally landed on Niihau over two hours after completing his attack on Bellows. Nishikaichi's plane and some of its fuel tanks had been hit by Bellows ground fire, but based on the aircraft's flight time, his fuel reserves remained adequate for an immediate return to *Hiryu*. Japanese aviators at this stage of the war were very well trained, and its hard to imagine Nishikaichi being unable to perform the relatively simple navigation problem required to find his way back to the fleet. Did a malfunctioning compass put him on the wrong heading? All we know is that after separating from his flight over Bellows, his presence was not reported again until the crash on Niihau hours later.

---

28   Aylmer Robinson letter to G. Allen, July 23, 1948, Hawaii War Records, University of Hawaii, Manoa campus

The burned out cockpit/rear fuselage viewed from just behind the engine.
Photo: Craig Barnum Collection

The exact method used by Nishikaichi and Harada to set the Zero alight is also a mystery. There are no specific details found either in the Mizuha or Baldwin reports, and no islander has since reported witnessing the steps used to ignite it. Examination of the post fire photographs and the surviving wreckage offers only incomplete clues. Rev. Denise's photos show extreme fire damage from the "accessory case" area immediately behind the engine, through the cockpit, and extending into the empennage just short of the tail. With no fuel left in the tanks to burn, the only accelerant still aboard would have been in the engine's oil tank, mounted just forward of the cockpit and its fuselage fuel tank. The gallons of oil still in the tank could have been drained and then poured into the cockpit to fuel the fire, or dried brush could have been put in the cockpit as tinder, with the resulting fire eventually igniting the oil tank's contents. We may never know what happened, but the oil tank's involvement in the fire is quite evident by the near total incineration of the area surrounding its location.

Keith Robinson offered this opinion in a 2013 interview with the author: "Dead, dried kiawe wood is abundant on Niihau, and burns with great heat. Since there was no electricity in Puuwai village at that time, each house had a pile of kiawe nearby for heating water or cooking. Since the villagers had now fled, all that Harada and Nishikaichi would have had to do is steal this firewood from the nearest house (*Hawila Kaleohano's*), pile it in the plane and light it."

The surviving wing fuel tank areas show no sign of fire, only the upper sections of the forward spar area that integrated with the cockpit structure above it show heat damage. In the Zero's construction, the wings and cockpit are built as a unified component, and only after the cockpit burned away could the wings be pulled apart as shown in Denise's photos. After the fire consumed all the oil and any other combustibles within the fuselage, it simply burned itself out.

Did The Niihau event contribute in any way to President Roosevelt's February 19, 1942, signing of Executive Order 9066, leading to the internment/relocation of Japanese nationals and Japanese-Americans during WWII? As stated in the previous chapter, this claim lacks factual support. KT's own exhaustive research including working with archivists at the Franklin D. Roosevelt Presidential Library, located no documents establishing a connection. The earliest Niihau-related item found in the President's papers was a letter dated March 6, 1942, from Representative S.W. King of Hawaii, recommending a Presidential commendation for heroic actions by Benjamin Kanahele and his wife against an enemy pilot. Harada's involvement was not mentioned in the letter but a newspaper clipping from a Honolulu newspaper about the event had been enclosed. This letter post-dates the EO 9066 signing by nearly a month.

Even the United States Naval Intelligence Service investigation report written by Captain Mayfield ("Japanese Residents of T.H.- Loyalty of") which is reproduced in Part I of this book, was not found among Roosevelt's papers. This report was defined in *Pearl Harbor: Final Judgement* by H. Clausen and B. Lee as an "inter-staff routing slip." Captain Mayfield's report and the Office of Naval Intelligence report originally attached to it is also absent from Roosevelt's archive. There is simply no written documentation in the archives indicating that Roosevelt had ever seen them. Extrapolating that the Mayfield report influenced EO 9066 is a common but flawed perception. There is no evidence the report made it to the White House, even though it was written weeks before EO 9066 had been signed.

An FBI report from J. Edgar Hoover about the event was sent to the President Roosevelt via the Secretary of the President (Major

General Edwin M. Watson), and was received on March 23, 1942 (see appendix 6). This too was after EO 9066's signing. The decision making process leading to EO 9066 had already evolved before written word of the Niihau event reached the President's office.

Racial prejudice and wartime hysteria did quickly ramp up in America against anyone of Japanese ancestry as the *Civil Liberties Act of 1988* states- particularly after the Pearl Harbor attack and the dark first years of the war. There is no debating that reality, and since the Niihau event was in no way a component of EO 9066's gestation, the default explanation for the now despised Executive Order's existence relies on the reasons declared in the *Civil Liberties Act* itself. However, additional insights beyond the *Commission of Wartime Relocation and Internment of Civilians* conclusions (whose findings lead to the *Civil Liberties Act of 1988*) may suggest further possibilities.

David Lowman, a former Special Assistant to the Director of the National Security Agency, presents alternative perspectives [29]. Lowman describes how the U.S. Army Signal Intelligence Service broke Japan's highest level diplomatic code in late 1940, allowing them to read Japan's transmitted diplomatic traffic until the end of the war. The intelligence gained from this ability was itself code named "MAGIC" by the American code breakers. There were over 5,000 messages decoded, originating from Berlin, Moscow, China, Central and South America, Mexico, Thailand, New York, Washington D.C., and Tokyo among others. A number of those intercepted during 1941 indicate Imperial Japan's wide net of espionage interests on America's west coast. Along with numerous supporting documents, photographs and references, Lowman also presents a number of actual "MAGIC" interceptions in his book- all originally classified and hidden away since WWII until the 1966 *Freedom of Information Act* eventually released them to the National Archives [30].

The following is an example of one of the 1941 MAGIC intercepts dated seven months before the Pearl Harbor attack.

---

29 MAGIC—The Untold Story of U.S. Intelligence and the Evacuation of Japanese
  Residents from the West Coast During WWII, David Lowman, Athena Press
30 Department of Defense publication "The 'MAGIC' Background of Pearl Harbor,"1977

FROM: Los Angeles (Nakuauchi)
May 9, 1941
TO: Tokyo (Gaimudaijin)
#067.
(In 2 parts- complete),
Strictly Secret.
Re your message # 180 to Washington.

We are doing everything in our power to establish outside contacts in connection with our
efforts to gather intelligence material. In this
regard, we have decided to make use of white
persons and Negros, through Japanese persons
whom we can't trust completely. (It not only
would be very difficult to hire U.S. (military?)
experts for this work at the present time, but
the expenses would be exceedingly high.) We
shall, furthermore, maintain close connections
with the Japanese Association, the Chamber of
Commerce, and the newspapers.
    With regard to airplane manufacturing
plants and other military establishments in other parts, we plan to establish very close relations with various organizations and in strict
secrecy have them keep these military establishments under close surveillance. Through such
means, we hope to be able to obtain accurate
and detailed intelligence reports. We have already established contacts with absolutely re-
liable Japanese in the San Pedro and San Diego
area, who will keep close watch on all shipments
of airplanes and other war materials, and report
the amounts and destinations of such shipments.
The same steps have been taken with regard to
traffic across the U.S.- Mexican border. We shall
maintain connection with our second generations
who are at present in the (U.S.) Army, to keep
us informed of various developments in the Army.
We also have connections with our second genera-

tions working in airplane plants for intelligence purposes.

With regard to the Navy, we are cooperating with our Naval Attache's office, and are submitting reports as accurately and as speedily as possible.

We are having Nakazawa investigate and summarize information gathered through first hand and newspaper reports, with regard to military movements, labor disputes, communistic activities and other similar matters. With regard to anti-Jewish movements, we are having investigations made by both prominent Americans and Japanese who are connected with the movie industry which is centered in this area. We have already established connections with very influential Negros to keep us informed with regard to the Negro movement [31].

Lowman's opinion was that these MAGIC interceptions were the real underlying reason for the large scale displacement of both Japanese nationals and Japanese- Americans from the west coast during the war. The ethnic Japanese population by chance had unfortunately settled coastal areas near important shipping ports, military installations and war production factories. The government and its intelligence agencies did not want to show their hand by announcing they had broken the diplomatic codes and were listening in on the transmissions, so other reasons for internment or relocation were invented.

Lowman states that the Commission's *(Commission on Wartime Internment and Relocation of Citizens)* two-year long study was corrupted by internal bias, pressures from influential political action

---

31   Department of Defense publication "The "MAGIC" Background of Pearl Harbor" 1977, National Archives, and "MAGIC-The untold story of U.S. Intelligence and the Evacuation of Japanese residents from the West Coast during WWII", Lowman, Athena Press

groups seeking redress, and sympathetic politicians. One of his biggest assertions is that the MAGIC documents were not considered during the process, and remained completely unknown to many of the Commission's members. Without the intelligence component from the MAGIC intercepts, the Commission ultimately (and in Lowman's opinion, incorrectly) defined the reasons for the internment/relocation event as purely racist.

This author makes no claims in support or against Mr. Lowman's work; his book and its supporting documents must speak for themselves. The eight-volume, Department of Defense publication *The "Magic" Background of Pearl Harbor* presents the original, de-encrypted messages without any commentary or interpretation. Those who are inclined toward further reading on the subject may want to study both these resources as well as those detailing the Japanese national/Japanese-American experience in America during WWII, and come to their own conclusions.

Many decades and several generations now lie between the events of WWII and today, and America now is a much different place. The legendary "Purple Heart Battalion" (100th Battalion) and the "Go For Broke" 442nd Combat Regiment both comprised of American *Nisei,* have rightly come to exemplify Japanese-American patriotism, bravery and sacrifice during that time period. Their contributions, as well as those of their like-minded civilian and other military brethren, speak far louder even today than anomalies like Yoshio Harada.

So why did Harada make the decision to take Aylmer's shotgun, to free Nishikaichi and join with him in threatening the Niihau people? Without him being here to answer directly, perhaps the best answer we have is in combining one of Irene Harada's statements in her Japanese television interview and a portion of the final sentence on the subject in the *Encyclopedia of Japanese American History:*

"Because Harada was a Japanese too, he decided to help Nishikaichi. Harada knew that there would be consequences for this act." *-Irene Harada, 1991*

and

"...because of the unusual conditions on Niihau..."- *Encyclopedia of Japanese American History*

EPILOGUE

By Keith Robinson, co-owner of Niihau Island

Benehakaka Kanehele (often called "Benny" or "Bene" in official reports and newspaper accounts) had already died years earlier, in the late 1950s or early 1960s. Part of the reason for his death may have been that he fell asleep on a honey wagon that weighed 4000 pounds (about 1000 pounds each wheel). Toppling off, he fell into the road, and one of the wheels passed directly over his head.

He did not even lose consciousness-in fact, he seemed totally unharmed by the incident, but after that, Aylmer Robinson thought that Benny seemed to age faster than is normal.

Hifuo "Jack" Mizuha proved the truth of the old adage that "you can't keep a good man down." After being temporarily demoted in the anti-Japanese hysteria that followed Pearl Harbor, he went on to have an extremely successful and honored career. He eventually retired as a justice of the Hawaii State Supreme Court.

Joseph Keoua (Iokepa) Kelley (this last name is also sometimes spelled Kele in the official reports), the driver of the Cletrac during the furrow-plowing, continued to drive the Cletrac (and also trucks) during and after wartime years. He also sometimes served as a caretaker around the Robinson family house at Kiekie. He finally retired and died on Niihau.

Kauileilehua (Kaui) Keamoai, Kamakauliuli (Uliuli) Kawahalau, and Oliva Kamala, who had cleared brush and rolled boulders out of the way for the Cletrac during the furrow plowing, went on to other work. Kaui became an expert scout, checking livestock and waterholes for Niihau Ranch. Uliuli is believed to have helped Shintani with his bee-keeping.

Oliva Kamala took a slightly different track. He moved to Kauai, where he became a member of the Ditch Gang on the Robinson's sugar plantation. The Ditch Gang, despite its somewhat plebian name, was actually an elite group of expert, hand picked men, who regularly risked life and limb while tending the vital irrigation ditches in the sheer cliffs and precipitous canyons of West Kauai.

All three men finally retired to Robinson plantation housing on Kauai, and died there many years later.

Howell (Hawila) Kaleohano also later moved to Kauai, where he worked for years as a skilled stone-splitter, building irrigation ditches on the Robinson's sugar plantation, before his eventual retirement and death. His son, Howell Kaleohano Jr., became a sergeant in the Hawaii Army National Guard, and a sub-foreman on the Robinson sugar plantation. His grandson, Howell Kaleohano III, recently retired as a respected and well-liked officer in the Kauai Police Department. He still lives at Waimea, Kauai, near the place where his famous grandfather and the five other heroic Niihau men came ashore on December 13, 1941, after their exhausting and extremely dangerous whale boat trip across the Niihau channel.

Like Howell (Hawila) Kaleohano, all of the other five members of the whale boat crew have now passed on - the three Kaohelaulii brothers (Kekuhina, Enoka, and Akana) are dead as is their relative (cousin?) Billie Kaohelaulii, and Kahokuloa Kanahele. They in their turn had risen on Niihau as the years passed. Kekuhina remained one of the two top men on Niihau, and later was succeeded by his younger brother Akana, who had formerly pulled one of the bow oars in the Niihau whale boat, and had later become the foreman of the Niihau cowboys. Akana died suddenly on January 1, 1975, probably from a heart attack.

Kahokuloa Kanahele became one of Niihau's few truck drivers. For years not many men were entrusted with Niihau's few, precious trucks partly because of the naturally rugged terrain, and partly because of those awful, vehicle eating furrows.

Enoka Kaohelaulii also sometimes served as a Niihau truck driver in later years. His son Hoa retired from the Robinson sugar plantation some years ago, and still lives in its housing on west Kauai.

Major Gerald Clark Brant never lost his obsession in trying to prevent the coming Pearl Harbor disaster. In 1939, by then reportedly a Brigadier General, he is said to have laid out a full size map replica of Pearl Harbor on the bed of a California dry lake. He then accurately bombed it, while personally leading a formation of attack planes. But even then no one listened to his claim that such an air raid was possible.

During World War II Brant rose to the rank of Major General (two stars). It is believed that he would have gotten a third star, if he hadn't damaged his career in the 1920s when he was only a lowly Major, by bravely supporting Mitchell against the U.S. Army's top brass, during Mitchell's famous court-martial. A bad heart finally killed him in the middle 1940s: but he still lives on in distant background legends, as the originator of the Robinson family's national defense work. Brant's grandson, Phillip Brant, still lives in Texas, in the same area where his grandfather retired.

Mitsuo Fuchida, the leader of Japan's air armada at Pearl Harbor, was converted to Christianity by an American ex-POW. He eventually became a Christian minister, and later met Rev. Paul Denise while the two men were attending an evangelical conference on the mainland USA. While the two were swapping war stories, Fuchida confirmed that there had indeed been a Japanese lifeguard submarine stationed off Niihau on December 7, 1941. Paul Denise in turn passed that information to Keith Robinson in 1978.

Reverend Paul Denise finally retired to New York and Florida, but returned occasionally to Kauai in his later years. Like almost all of the other participants in the Niihau incident, he eventually died without telling even his closest descendants about the details of that affair, or his part in it.

After his WWII internment, little Ishimatsu Shintani (he was only five feet tall) was gladly welcomed back to Niihau, where he resumed his former energetic work as Niihau's head beekeeper. He proved irreplaceable; after he retired, Niihau's honey and beeswax production ended within a few years. Also after that, a noxious, thorny and highly invasive weed (Lantana camara) soon overran Niihau. Niihau was the last main Hawaiian island to be thus infested, many years after the others were already covered with it. This is dramatic proof of just how hard Shintaini and his three sons had worked, even during their extra time when the weren't tending bees. Up to that time, the entire 72 square mile island had been kept totally free of lantana - whenever the Shintanis heard of even one bush somewhere, they had immediately gone out to uproot it.

During his retirement years Ishimatsu Shintani moved to a house he owned at Kekaha, Kauai, right across the channel from Niihau. From there, now in his eighties, he often walked in the hot sun to get his mail at the Makaweli Post Office - each round trip covered about ten miles and took two hours.

Finally, now in his very last years he had a brief siege of illness that temporarily put him into Mahelona Hospital on Kaui's east side, some forty or forty five miles from his Kekaha house. Shortly after that Keith Robinson got a panicky call from a nurse in Mahelona.

"Mr. Robinson," the frightened woman said, "Mr. Shintani has recovered, and is being discharged right now. But we are all really scared. At the moment there is no one to drive him home, and he says that's no problem, he'll just walk."

"Mr. Shintani is taking it very calmly, except that he appears really set on walking home. But he's almost ninety, and we're really badly worried . What on earth should we do?"

To which Keith Robinson replied, "I know that man well, and he means what he says! He'll do it too - it will take him fifteen or twenty hours, but he'll do it! Hold him there - whatever you do, hold him, don't turn him loose! Tell him I'm coming right this minute with a car!"

Shintaini's oldest son Kuramatsu eventually became the foreman of Niihau's charcoal gang, in the years when Niihau produced large amounts of high grade Kiawe charcoal. He eventually died early in 2013, shortly before his 90th birthday. Like his father, he was still going alone all over Niihau, but now on a bicycle.

Most of Shintaini's other descendants still live on Niihau, and also all over western Kauai.

According to a semi-legend among the Niihau cowboys, Aylmer Robinson rode his last bucking horse at the age of 75. Nobody had planned it that way. The horse was believed to be a quiet one, but it blew up just as he was climbing into the saddle.

He never did manage to get into the saddle, but he did cling to the side of the furiously bucking horse for a hundred yards, before finally coming off. Furthermore - and this really impressed the cowboys - *he came off standing up.*

Three years later he was dead of cancer, but right up to the end, even only two weeks before he died, he was secretly dragging himself out of bed to work in his office at night. Aylmer Francis Robinson died in 1967 at the age of 78, and his younger brother Lester Beauclerk Robinson (the father of Keith and Bruce Robinson) likewise passed away two years later in 1969, at the age of 68.

These were the kinds of people that were involved in the Niihau incident.

Keith and Bruce Robinson, as the present owners of Niihau, still maintain their traditional close association with the Niihau islanders. They are also continuing their efforts to preserve Niihau as their ancestors and King Kamehemeha V would have wanted.

Both brothers have sometimes been described as men with one foot in the American Frontier, and one foot in the Space Age. They are thoroughly familiar with the realities of the present: but they also vividly remember and respect the religion, history and morals of their ancestors, as well as the aboriginal language, history, and culture of Niihau.

Both can easily slip back into the simple life of an earlier time. When Hurricane Iniki devastated Kauai in 1992, knocking out power for days, both men happily re-adapted to wood fires, kerosene lanterns and the blessed absence of televised news scandals and endlessly ringing telephones.

APPENDIX 1

THEY COULDN'T TAKE NIIHAU NO-HOW

Words and music by R. Alex Anderson 1943

On the tiny island of Niihau, no one knew a war was on
Til a Japanese flier decided to retire and landed with a machine gun.
Then a big Ben Kanahele laid aside his ukulele
He told the aviator he would throw him in the crater

If he didn't get the heck right out
But the Jap shot Ben in the shoulder, in the ribs and in the groin
Kanahele took a swallow and tightened up his malo
And the he girded up his other loin

Then big Kanahele grabbed the Jap around the belly
And threw him down against a stone wall
And Mrs. Kanahele took a rock and made a jelly of his head
Til he was dead and that was all

Chorus:

So they couldn't take Niihau no-how and with the Ben Kanaheles around
The Jap was a sap to think it a snap
When he set his airplane down
So they couldn't take Niihau no-how
When big Kanahele said "pau"!
He made a grand slam for his Uncle Sam and
They couldn't Take Niihau no-how

APPENDIX 2

Niihau Zero crash site archaeological mapping plan

Syd Jones

12/20/05

This privately owned island with its unique cultural and biological sensitivities requires a very light footprint by survey and recovery teams. All activities must be designed to be the **least intrusive possible**. This bias must take precedence over any data collection or artifact recovery plans. It is also understood that the integrity of this aircraft crash site was disturbed originally during efforts by the U.S. military to remove the engine, propeller and other components of interest to national security. This crude disassembly produced a secondary scatter of site artifacts

Another significant artifact on Niihau is a tractor/plow purchased by the island owners to furrow large portions of the island, denying its use as an airfield. This was reportedly done in direct response to an interwar paper by Gen. Billy Mitchell. He predicted an eventual conflict with Japan where they would attack Pearl Harbor on a Sunday morning. Gen. Mitchell felt that Niihau might be used by the Japanese as a stage area for their attack. The Robinson family, at their own expense, sought to eliminate this possibility by purchasing the tractor and using it to defile any airfield possibilities.

These two artifact groups will require separate methodologies to understand. The Zero aircraft deposit is the more complex.

AIRCRAFT CRASH SITE PROCEDURE:

A) Establish the original resting spot of the Zero before its U.S.

dissection. Since an attempt was made by the pilot to burn the aircraft shortly after the crash, melted aluminum will be evident where this happened. A large part of the cockpit and rear fuselage was rendered down by fire so there should be ample evidence of melted small puddles of aluminum on or into the ground.

Aluminum is especially easy to locate with metal detectors, so this area (if near to the currently surviving Zero structure) should be discernible. Once located, a survey benchmark would be established on the spot. Through physical, photographic evidence and Robinson family interviews, establishing the original fore-aft axis of the aircraft would be attempted.

B) Segregate primary from secondary scatter. Interviews with Robinson family members may help to determine the path of the initial impact and skid to the original Dec. 7, 1941 resting position. Examination of the local rocks and terrain for scarring could provide supporting evidence as well. Fragments found along the crash run out up to this 12/7/41 location including the melted aluminum will be considered primary scatter material. All structure displaced from this location by the later U.S. removal of components will be considered secondary scatter.

C) All artifacts located and marked for site mapping. All artifacts located either visually or with detector are to be marked in situ for site mapping and given permanent, sequentially numbered tags. Digital photographs depicting relationships of major artifact groupings, large or identifiable artifacts and site relationship overviews will be made before and during site mapping. Survey controls will be by GPS and radial distance representations around benchmarks, not to exceed 75 feet without establishment of another GPS benchmark. Ground slope and notable terrestrial features, large rocks, trees, fence lines etc. relating to the crash site will be mapped in using GPS with benchmark tie-ins where applicable. Notes will be made on site determining primary or secondary status for each artifact. A small soil sample from the vicinity of larger artifacts to be taken for PH, moisture analysis (metal degradation studies) purposes.

D) As site mapping progresses a plan for recovery of artifacts can be finalized. Small artifacts will be gathered in containers for bulk removal while larger may be cargo netted for helicopter lift.

E) A site map presenting all data recorded will be generated as a permanent record for analysis and education of the wreck's nature.

Questions to be answered by aircraft crash site inspection.

1. What was the location and heading direction of the aircraft's landing run out? **Terrestrial, Interview**
2. What was the appeal of the selected landing site's location? **Aerial**
3. A fence was reputed to snag the landing gear, tearing them off. What type of fence, how was it situated relative to the run out heading and is there any portion surviving. How far from where the aircraft came to rest was this fence? An intact wire type (barbed wire?) fence appears in close proximity to the aircraft in an original photograph. Was this the fence? In this type of incident, any sudden, significant drag on the landing gear during landing almost certainly assures the tailwheel type aircraft flipping on its back rather than simply tearing off the gear. Original photographs of the aircraft show this did not happen. Is there any evidence remaining to indicate why? **Terrestrial, Interview**
4. Did the aircraft hold its heading orientation during the entire landing runout or did it rotate along its axis. If so what possible obstacles are evident that would have imparted this rotation. **Terrestrial, Interview**
5. Is there any ground scarring evident? How long is the run out track? **Terrestrial, Interview**
6. What is the slope and ground surface type along the primary impact and scatter trail. **Terrestrial**

7. What evidence exists of the U.S. recovery of selected components (discarded mechanical hardware, etc., displacement of surviving structures. **Terrestrial**

TRACTOR/PLOW PROCEDURE

A) GPS position and orientation of tractor to be noted. Since it is not known at this writing as to whether the tractor was used for any other services post the island furrowing, its current location may or may not be of importance. Digital photographs will be made of the artifacts on site. During the inspection plans for recovery can be finalized, possibly by high lift helicopter. **Terrestrial, Interview**

B) Surviving furrow depth, orientation and extent to be noted. Spot measurements as practical will be made. Digital photographs from the surface as well as from the air will be taken to understand the parameters and effectiveness of this activity. **Terrestrial, Interview, Aerial.**

C) Interview of Robinson family representatives is crucial in understanding the time period and impetus for their accomplishing this expensive and time consuming activity. **Interview**

D) A furrowing site map of Niihau will be generated. This information will be based on aerial photographs and Robinson family information and will show the approximate extent and orientation of their completed furrow project. **Aerial, Interview**

APPENDIX 3

Note: The photos imbedded in this letter were added by Syd Jones, and were sourced from the National Park Service and Craig Barnum Collections, which also document the discussed events.

From Keith Robinson
To: Syd Jones
August 9, 2013

Dear Syd
        Here is what I know about the events of December 16, 1941 on Niihau.
        Early that morning a party of military men sailed from Kauai to Niihau, aboard two commandeered sampans, for the purpose of inspecting Nishikaichi's Zero, and taking parts and samples from it. The Robinson's sampan "Lehua" was probably one of them.

Robinson sampan "Lehua" off northern Niihau viewed from the second sampan.
Photo: National Park Service 539.1

Uncle Aylmer and Reverend Paul Denise (pronounced Dee-Nice) were aboard the vessels. (I presume that they were together in on of the boats, since the two men were good friends, and Denise, by his own later statement, was specifically invited along as Uncle Aylmer's "guest").

But there was a lot more to it than that. Denise, who was an excellent amateur photographer, had somehow been hastily recruited by the military to be the expedition's photographer. He was now loaded with camera film (he would reportedly take more than 500 pictures that day), and he had apparently also been given a temporary military commission and a military uniform.

There can only have been one reason for that. The military obviously considered this to be a high-risk mission: and Denise (the pastor of a church at Waimea, Kauai) was being given a temporary military status, so that he would at least be protected under the Geneva Convention if captured by the enemy.

Reverend Denise (second from left) on Niihau with the Army Zero evaluation team. Photo: Craig Barnum Collection

This action by the U.S. military, in giving Denise that uniform, speaks far more loudly than any words. It clearly corroborates what all the old-timers have told me, that by then even the U.S. military feared a Japanese invasion of Hawaii at any moment.

Rev. Denise with the Army Zero salvage team on Niihau armed with a Browning Automatic Rifle. Photo: Craig Barnum Collection

But Aylmer Robinson, a genuine, lifelong conscientious objector, would have refused to wear a uniform, even under those desperate circumstances, when it would have been clearly to his advantage to do so.

The man was no coward - in fact, he was extraordinarily brave: but he had extremely deep moral and religious convictions, which he carefully kept private and almost never discussed with anyone.

Preparing "Lehua" for the trip to Niihau, probably the morning before departure. Photo: National Park Service 539.8

The two sampans were escorted on their trip by a single PBY flying boat circling overhead - a pathetically weak escort, but all that could be spared in those first desperate days after Pearl Harbor.

The little convoy apparently set off from West Kauai sometime in the pre-dawn hours of December 16, probably 3:30-5:30 A.M.

By sunrise they were apparently approaching

Lehua Channel, or had just gone through it. It is not known where they planned to go next. The Kaununui and Nonopapa landings were the closest to the wrecked plane: but if any winter surf was running, both would have been unusable.

However, later events during the day suggest that there was no really big surf at the time, and that Kaununui and Nonopapa might have been usable. But fate evidently decreed otherwise.

Zero salvage party aboard "Lehua" in the sheltered waters near Niihau.
Photo: National Park Service 539.22

The convoy was just in Lehua Channel, or just emerging from its southwestern end, when (according to several Niihau witnesses and also Rev. Denise) the PBY escort spotted and attacked a Japanese submarine lurking in the waters west and southwest of Lehua Island.

The PBY attack on the submarine is said to have been independently witnessed by Niihau men working at the following widely separated locations:

1)   A party of men somewhere in Lehue Land. These would have been no more that 2-3 miles away, at most.

2)   A gang of men working to clear a cattle driving trail from the Niihau mountains down to the Kaununui flatlands, probably at an elevation of about 400-600 feet, about 1-2 miles southwest of Mokouia Valley. These men, although about 3 miles from the incident, would have had an excellent overlook for viewing the entire affair. Furthermore, the day was clear, the light was good, and Niihau men are noted for the sharpness of their vision.

3)   An observer (Kaui Keamoai ?) on the low promontory above the sea just above and outside of Loe waterhole, some 3-4 miles to the southwest.

In addition to the Niihau observers, Rev. Paul Denise was aboard one of the sampans (probably the Robinsons' sampan, "Lehua", named after the rough waters east and north of Lehua Island): and Denise very definitely and personally told me in 1978, that the PBY had spotted and attacked a submarine. Also, the fact that Uncle Aylmer and Denise were probably together, throughout that day and the following night, and on the trip back to Kauai the next day, strongly supports the theory that Aylmer Robinson likewise was fully aware of the attack on the sub.

If the whole thing had been a false alarm, Uncle Aylmer would almost certainly have told Denise, and Denise never would have spent the rest of his life falsely imagining an encounter between the PBY and the sub. Furthermore, the place where the PBY is said to have started its attack on the submarine was only a mile (or a little more) distant from the two sampans: and the waters immediately west and southwest of Lehua, sheltered by the island's bulk, are usually very calm in a normal tradewind conditions.

Over and above all this, Denise was the expedition's photographer: and he is known to have taken over 500 pictures that day, most of which have never been seen by even his closest relatives. Did he get his camera out in time to record the action, or was the incident over too quickly (cameras are extremely sensitive to salt spray, and it would have taken Denise at least 1-3 minutes to unpack it from its special ocean-going wrappings).

There are some odd aspects of the story that don't add up, at least not in my mind.

While it was nowhere explicitly stated by the Niihau men, the few accounts they ever gave seem to suggest that the submarine was partly or fully surfaced. This is odd, especially when one considers that the encounter between the PBY and the sub seems to have occurred at or just after sunrise.

Why would a sub be sitting on the surface at that hour, in almost full daylight? Was it partly surfaced, with its deck barely awash, so that it could listen for the radio signals from downed aviators?

HOWEVER...the waters immediately adjacent to the sheer west wall of Lehua Island are probably the best place in all Hawaii to hide a surfaced submarine. No ordinary naval commander would ever dream of looking for a sub in that place. In less than one hundred yards offshore (perhaps even as little as 100 feet) the water depth is seven hundred feet, and a gray submarine would be extremely difficult to see against the brownish-gray background of Lehua Island's sheer western sea cliffs.

In fact, even the Niihau people themselves do not seem to have noticed it before the PBY finally spotted it and attacked. And the PBY itself, circling over the two sampans, would never have seen the sub hidden behind Lehua Island, not until the sampans were in Lehua Channel, or even at it western exit. So it is possible that the sub commander, knowing that the Americans were totally focused on trying to salvage and defend Pearl Harbor, complacently assumed that no one would ever see him in his snug hidey-hole.

And normally he would have been absolutely correct in that assumption. But he had no idea that a freak, one in a million combination of circumstances was bringing a PBY toward him: and it must have come as a nasty shock when the PBY suddenly emerged from behind the towering Lehua Island Cliff, which hid it until it was almost directly overhead.

What happened next is totally unclear – there are several versions, most of which say the sub was sunk after a brief flight.Denise himself never told me – as soon as he realized that Dad and Uncle Aylmer had never told me a word about the sub and the PBY, he himself clammed up and I never got another word out of him about what happened between the sub and the PBY.

So all I know from Denise is that the PBY found a sub, and attacked it, and then crashed. I got the fleeting impression that Denise thought the PBY might have sunk the sub, but he just wouldn't tell me anything. But the Niihau people's various versions of the events do give the general impression that the sub was sunk or damaged. Either way, it disappeared underwater, and was not seen again.

One version of the story says that quite a lot of oil came up at that time, and for weeks thereafter oil came up from a certain spot offshore, until seepage finally stopped after a violent winter-spring storm in early 1942. Who knows what really happened. Aylmer Robinson and Paul Denise and all the Niihau witnesses are long dead.

But no one disputes (and the official record confirms) that the PBY crashed immediately afterward. The official record says that it hit a wind shear and spun downward into the water: the Niihau version says it was damaged in the fight with the sub, but managed to struggle something like a mile toward land, before crashing in shallow water about a quarter mile offshore.

The PBY apparently impacted nose-first at a fairly steep angle, splitting the nose open, and killing the pilot and copilot, whose bodies were never recovered.

All the rest of the crew survived: but most reportedly had major impact injuries - only one or two men emerged intact from the wreck.

The nose of the PBY sank until it came to rest on the shallow ocean floor, but for some reason the tail of the plane trapped some air, and remained floating at the sea surface, probably for several hours.

This fact saved the lives of the PBY survivors, who had gotten into the plane's yellow life raft, but (probably due to their injuries, and the prevailing wind) were unable to paddle upwind to shore.

So - to prevent themselves from being blown

helplessly offshore to certain death in the open ocean – the clung to the plane's floating tail. There was nothing else they could do, but hang onto the plane's tail and hope that it wouldn't sink.

Meanwhile, observing this potential disaster, the Niihau men swiftly decided on a rescue: but it would take hours to execute.

First, men had to race several miles on horseback to the Puuwai-Kiekie area. There they grabbed the Cletrac tractor, and hitched a trailer cart to it.

Onto this trailer they put a small, ancient Hawaiian outrigger canoe, which the Cletrac towed several miles northward at full speed over rough bouncy terrain (not good for the Cletrac, the canoe, or the trailer).

Then the canoe was launched and the Niihau people paddled out, rescued the PBY survivors, and brought them ashore.

The fact that this little outrigger canoe was successfully launched at that spot, strongly suggests that there wasn't much surf on the northwestern coast of Niihau that morning, and that the Nonopapa and Kaununui landings were calm.

Meanwhile, the rest of the expedition was proceeding with its assigned mission to recover parts from the Zero.

But by now Aylmer Robinson was almost certainly extremely worried.

According to the information he had gotten from Mitchell via Brant on 1933, Niihau Island would be the first Hawaiian island the Japanese would invade, in their operation to seize the Hawaiian islands.

But the seizure of Niihau would also involve an air attack on Pearl Harbor, on a Sunday morning, beginning around 7:30 A.M.

Now just such a highly successful surprise attack had indeed occurred, almost exactly as Mitchell and Brant predicted.

Furthermore, other highly successful Japanese invasions (including the December 10 seizure of Guam) were already occurring elsewhere in the Pacific.

And the presence of a Japanese submarine close offshore of Niihau strongly suggested that the Japanese military might already be scouting the island, ahead of an oncoming invasion.

In other words, the Japanese might soon recover the remains of their warplane in an invasion landing. If the U.S. wanted to obtain any parts or samples from the plane, for technological analysis, the job would have to be done as quickly as possible, or the opportunity might be lost. But all kinds of unexpected delays and setbacks were already occurring.

The Nonopapa Landing and (especially) the Kaununui Landing were the closest ones to the wrecked Zero; from transportation and logistics standpoint, they would normally be the best and easiest ones to use; and furthermore (as already noted) surf conditions along the entire coastline were apparently fairly calm that morning.

But Nonopapa and (especially) Kaununui were dangerously exposed to possible attack, especially surprise attack by submarines. Kalani Hale, with its shallow offshore rocks and reefs, was slightly better protected. And also, with the PBY escort now gone, the two sampans carrying the expedition were almost totally defenseless.

So - Aylmer Robinson apparently decided to travel no further by sea down the sub-infested west coast of Niihau, but to land at Kaliani Hale up in the north, directly across from Lehua Island.

Rev. Denise on the beach near the old Kalani Hale landing.
Photo: Craig Barnum Collection

This was done. A picture taken at that time (apparently intended as a personal souvenir for Rev. Denise) clearly shows Denise standing on the beach in his military uniform, about a hundred yards north of the old Kalani Hale boat landing, with the western part of Lehua Island in the background.

But now - with no motorized transport available - the entire party would have to travel several extra miles by horseback to the wrecked Zero.

Several additional hours would now be needed for the round trip, to the Zero and back.

The delays were mounting up: and for all anyone knew, an oncoming Japanese invasion fleet might be as little as twenty or thirty hours away.

Little is now known about the following hours. No one involved ever talked or left any written records.

But tantalizing bits of circumstantial evidence do give strong clues about what happened

The Army Zero salvage team riding across central Niihau's Karrawea sand country, about 10:00 am on Dec.16,1941. Photo: National Park Service 539.21

Rev. Denise is said to have taken over 500 pictures of the wrecked Zero when he finally reached it.

I have seen a few of them: but the light and the angles in them strongly suggest that the party did not reach the Zero until sometime after noon of that day.

Meanwhile, the other members of the expedition, assisted by the Niihau people, started taking parts and samples from the Zero.

Surviving tool marks on the Zero's remains clearly show that this was no careful, leisurely disassembly. Instead, with time possibly running out, it was a frantic, smash-and-grab job.

The Zero wasn't disassembled, it was

stripped; it was butchered. The tool marks strongly suggest that things like hammers, cold chisels, hacksaws, and crowbars were repeatedly used that afternoon.

But the job wasn't done. Despite the fact that December 16 is on of the shortest days of the year, and that the expedition only had (at most) five or six hours of daylight left when they finally reached the Zero, they apparently accomplished all their objectives before the last light faded from the sky around 6:30 or 7:00 PM.

Recovered Zero parts loaded on a wagon photographed early on the morning of Dec.17, 1941 near Kalani Hale on Niihau's north shore, waiting to be picked up by "Lehua." Photo: National Park Service 539.23

But now they faced a long horseback ride at night, from Puuwai back to Kalani Hale at the north end of Niihau.

It must have been a night of a million fears.

There was no moon, and the ride was done by starlight (the moon was in its dark phase – the tiny crescent moon would not appear until two nights later, on December 18).

Also with a wartime blackout in effect, and a possible Japanese invasion fleet coming in the dark, and a large Japanese submarine (with its deck gun) possibly lurking offshore, no lights of any kind could be used in the work.

Furthermore, the northern part of Niihau can become quite cold on winter nights (the lowest temperature ever recorded on Niihau was 42 degrees Fahrenheit). Rev. Denise (a sometimes resident of upstate New York and no stranger to cold weather) has told me very clearly, that the night was bitterly cold.

But again, the job got done. Despite the dark and the cold, the entire salvage party - with all its metallurgical samples, and the Zero's engine, and the plane's propeller - successfully traversed the six or eight miles of rough terrain back to the north end of Niihau.

However, they may not have spent the rest of the night at the small, part-time family residence that the Robinsons then maintained at Kalani Hale. Instead, some circumstantial evidence (a photograph of mounted non-Niihau men on horseback, clearly taken at Nanina possibly the following morning) suggests that they may have gone instead to a small, inconspicuous shack at Nanina, some four hundred yards east-southeast of Kalani Hale.

The following morning, Dec. 17, another PBY came to Niihau from Oahu, and took the survivors of the Dec. 16 plane crash back to Oahu.

It is not known - but seems probable - that a third PBY may also have come along and provided cover for the two sampans as they returned to Kauai with the precious cargo.

But at any rate, with or without an escort, the two sampans returned uneventfully to Kauai.

And also after that - in other words, after December 17 - no submarines (and no mysterious lights offshore at night) seem to have ever again been seen by any Niihau people, for all the rest of World War Two.

This tallies rather well with a Japanese submarine history of World War Two, which states that a lifeguard submarine (the I-174) was stationed off Niihau for ten days, from Dec. 7 to Dec. 17, to rescue any downed aviators from Niihau.

But it is disputed by Mitsuo Fuchida's account, which states that the I-174 left the Niihau area during the afternoon of Dec. 7, 1941 and (supposedly) never returned.

Whose version of that submarine's activity is correct? Mitsuo Fuchida's memory, or the official historians of the World War II Japanese submarine service?

Again, no one today knows – everyone involved is probably long dead.

But one fact is certain in all of this.

The Niihau people (and Rev. Denise) had absolutely no advance knowledge of Japan's war plan to station a lifeguard submarine off of Niihau from Dec. 7 to Dec. 17, to rescue downed aviators.

And yet – they reported occasional mysterious lights offshore at night, and then finally even a submarine sighting, precisely in that exact time period.

But after that – never again. They never again reported anything like that, throughout all the rest of World War II.

So – were Aylmer Robinson, and Rev. Paul Denise, and some 6-12 Niihau men, all the victims of some kind of simultaneous mass delusion or hysteria, despite the fact that they witnessed the alleged encounter between the PBY and the submarine from at least four widely separated vantage points?

I flatly doubt that – I personally knew almost all of those men during their later lives, and not one of them ever impressed me a being prone to flights of fantasy.

Quite the opposite, in fact. Almost all of them had a very calm, skeptical, show-me-proof attitude about odd occurrences or rumors.

So - maybe the official Japanese submarine history was correct, and a Japanese submarine was in the area, just as Rev. Denise and all the Niihau people believed.

Now to summarize the events of Dec. 16-17, 1941 on Niihau.

Aylmer Robinson set out on an urgent expedition to photograph (and take parts from) what was then the most advanced type of warplane in the entire Pacific.

Time was of the essence: the job had to be done quickly, since a Japanese invasion was feared to be coming.

But he was dogged by bad luck and unexpected delays all through those desperate days; a submarine scare; the loss of his only Navy escort (the PBY); the rescue of injured aviators; the arranging of overnight shelter and care for badly injured men, on a cold night ; the late arrival at the Zero, with only a few hours of daylight left to do the work.

And finally, the black, cold nighttime horseback ride, for some 6-8 miles back north to Kalani Hale, with nobody knowing whether advance parties of Japanese had already landed, and were lying in ambush along the way.

It couldn't have been any fun at all, for anyone involved.

But... despite all the unexpected delays, and scares, and fears, and tension, and uncertainty- the job was successfully done.

Aylmer Robinson, ably assisted by his Niihau men and Rev. Denise, thoroughly photographed the Zero, and took all kinds of parts and samples from it for U.S. military intelligence.

They rescued some crashed and badly injured U.S. Navy flyers and cared for them throughout the following cold night, without losing a single man. And they did this right under the nose of a suspected Japanese invasion, which was believed to be impending at any moment (these fears did not subside in Hawaii, until after the Battle of Midway in 1942).

The thirty-six hours between the pre-dawn hours of Dec. 16, 1941, and the afternoon of the following day, when he returned to Kauai, must have been one of the toughest episodes of the Aylmer Robinson's entire life.

But (and this comes as no surprise to any one who knew the man), he got the job completely done.

It must have been one of his greatest personal triumphs, but he never spoke of it to anyone, throughout the rest of his life. In fact, he had been dead for eleven years before I first learned of the submarine scare off Niihau that day.

That pretty much summarizes what I know about the events of Dec. 16-17, 1941 on Niihau.

With warmest regards and best wishes,

Keith

Keith Robinson

APPENDIX 4

Preliminary analysis: A6M2 Zero primary and secondary sites and Cletrac artifacts and operational evidence on Niihau, Hawaii January 13, 2006.

By Syd Jones

After initial contacts made by Syd Jones through Allan Lloyd, Keith and Bruce Robinson agreed to a meeting with Allan Palmer, S. Jones and A. Lloyd to consider the placement of several artifacts located on Niihau in the Pacific Aviation Museum. The Japanese Zero which crashed there after attacking Oahu on December 7th 1941 was well documented at the time, with many parts recovered from it for technical analysis. Today the possibility of any surviving portions of the aircraft still being on the island is not known much beyond the Robinsons and the cloistered residents of Niihau.

Another fascinating artifact exists on the island. After a 1923-24 tour of the Pacific, air advocate Billy Mitchell predicted in his report that the U.S. and the Japanese would soon be at war. He felt that the Japanese would attack Oahu by air, using the island of Niihau as a staging area for their aircraft. A Lt. Col. Gerald C. Brant, who was stationed on Oahu in 1924-25 and again in 1930-34, was a firm believer in Mitchell's doctrine and contacted the Robinson family about altering the island so it could not be used for air operations.

According to Keith Robinson, the family started plowing furrows over the flat expanses over Niihau with oxen in 1937. Progress was too slow, so at their own expense the Robinson family imported a

Cletrac tractor from the mainland to expedite the process. To be effective, the furrows were made about 24 inches deep and about two and a half feet wide. The furrows were not just straight, parallel lines but a ninety degree cross hatch shape-forming squares about one hundred feet on a side. The project was completed in the summer of 1941 with much of the island being covered. Literally thousands of linear miles of furrows were done at the Robinson family's own expense.

The Cletrac tractor still resides on the island and it was reported that some of the furrowing still survives. The Japanese pilot, in looking for a landing spot for his Zero, had to avoid the cross-hatched area of furrows and chose to land on a boulder strewn rise instead.

On January 13, 2006 an inspection party from PAM flew via helicopter to Niihau with Keith Robinson acting as a guide. In anticipation of this event, an archaeological site mapping plan including a list of questions to be answered was developed by S. Jones in the hope of providing a framework to the brief visitation period of less than eight hours.

Basic survey equipment used included tape measures, survey stakes, compasses, tags, metal detectors, GPS, digital still and video cameras. It was known from the outset that the limited time allotted would severely inhibit the degree of data collection at the various locations to be examined.

In deference to the Robinson's request on our arrival, no photos or video were to be made of the inhabitants or their homes. This request was honored but understandably restricted the photo record of the original Zero crash site as a house and its stone perimeter fence has been built almost on top of the spot. GPS coordinates were taken at various positions of the Zero crash and storage sites for survey purposes but the Robinson's asked that these be deleted from our records.

The following locations were inspected in this order:

1. The current Zero artifacts resting spot (secondary site).

2. The original Zero crash location (primary site).

3. An area where the Zero was dragged to shortly after the crash.

4. The Cletrac and its plow.

5. A dry lake where cross hatching was still visible.

6. The beach opposite where a PBY crashed while escorting vessels from Kauai after the December 7th 1941 attack.

Zero Secondary Site

According to Keith Robinson, the Zero's surviving remains were collected up and deposited at this location two or three years prior. The landscape here is primarily flat, and semi–arid, overgrown with one meter high thorny plants known locally as "Sourgrass." The largest of the surviving structures had been laid out adjacent to each other with numerous unconsolidated fragments scattered around.

Though this was hardly an undisturbed feature, several methods were used to document this secondary scatter. A photo mosaic of the site was done and when completed two survey benchmarks biased along the axis of the artifact field were established to allow a quick triangulation of the major components. The benchmark distance and bearing were coupled with GPS coordinates (now deleted) at Position D on the Secondary Site Survey map.

The large pieces where given identifying tags with sequential numbers. After the photo mosaic and triangulation measurements were completed, the smaller unconsolidated fragments were gathered up and placed to the side to be tagged as a group for the present time. The large, tagged structures were placed to the side and the area where they had been sitting was examined with a VLF metal detector to locate any remaining fragments hidden by the overgrowth.

Time constraints allowed only a superficial examination of the surviving artifacts. This group appears to be the remains of the wings, primarily the area between the 20 mm. cannon wing mounts. Because much of the skin had been removed exposing the inner structure, the impression is that the remains are largely skeletal. The spar caps on both front and rear spars are completely reduced at all surviving locations, but overall much of the aluminum was still structurally viable.

Landing gear, wiring, flight control cables, pulleys, mechanical, hydraulic and electrical componentry are all absent. No part of the tail cone, horizontal or vertical stabilizers were noted in the limited time allotted. Evidence in the form of tool marks was visible from the crude original dismantling process. Much of the surviving external skin surfaces have red primer paint still showing, some internal pieces also displayed the greenish-blue tint primer. No components from the flight control surfaces were noted at the time.

One unexpected find was the apparent crushed aft tail cone of the center line fuel drop-tank. The presence of this artifact inspires more questions than answers. Why wasn't this tank dropped during combat or later when preparing for an emergency landing? If the tank couldn't be jettisoned for mechanical reasons, was this why the pilot chose to attempt a gear down landing on an unknown surface?

The Zero pilot attempted to burn the aircraft as events unfolded after the crash. This fire consumed the cockpit area and a portion of the aft fuselage before it went out by itself. The spar carry through under the cockpit show distortion from melting and a piece of the port lower forward cockpit skin complete with engine mount structure and firewall fragments shows the same.

One 4-foot (plus) portion of an outer wing remains, what has survived is captured between the front and rear spars. Other spar web fragments were found – all missing the spar caps and the rivets that would have held them together. One notable fragment is believed to be an aileron "well" at the trailing edge of the wing. It still has a long, thin piece of wood strip affixed with ferrous screws as an apparent chaffing guard.

While finishing up the plotting tasks, one of the Niihau guides (Gilbert K. Pohulelua) brought over a corroded radial engine blower case that had been kept in another location. The case had several sections sawed out of it and had surface corrosion to the extent that no casting or other markings could be seen. It could not be ascertained at the initial inspection whether this item was in fact from the Zero or from one of the other period crashes known to have happened on the island. The component was from a twin row fourteen cylinder engine like the Sakae 12.

Research upon returning to Honolulu indicates that this is in fact the engine blower case from the crashed Zero. The engine evidently was completely taken apart for inspection on the island and only certain parts removed.

Plots of the major artifact features have been represented on the Secondary Site Survey map which includes a preliminary identification of their components. The photo mosaic of the site was assembled to compliment this information. The aircraft artifacts were left in situ.

Zero Primary Site

It was hoped that the crash site of the Zero was still basically an open area with little change since 1941. Prior to this visit to Niihau, some effort had been made to find some original photos of the wreck before it was disturbed. When some pictures were finally found, a number of distant and near landmarks were noted to try and establish the exact present location. If the original resting spot could be located, there was a good chance that evidence would be found about the nature of the last seconds of the flight as well as fragments from the aircraft.

The original fence line of wire and natural wooden posts still existed in its 1941 location (repaired and replaced over the years). The Zero had plowed through this light barrier and skidded to an abrupt halt amongst the large lava boulders scattered on the ground. Unfortunately, a recently built house, a stone fence and the graded lot within now occupies the likely spot where the aircraft came to rest.

A ridge line descending onto a sandy plain, trees (now dead) on the ridgeline and the wire and post fence line are all still surviving elements in the post crash pictures visible today. Several local Niihau residents that were accompanying our party as well as Keith Robinson all stated that the aircraft had come to rest just about or inside where the stone fence had been built. By comparing the background views in the vintage photos, their opinions seemed very accurate.

Unfortunately, the large uniquely shaped boulders that lay in the foreground of the photos had apparently been moved to build the stone wall and to clear the way for an access road that now runs along the wire fence. Had they still been there, pinpointing the exact spot would have been much easier. An inspection of the whole area only confirmed that the Zero's final movement stopped within the immediate vicinity of the new stone wall. (See Position A, Primary Site Survey (GPS deleted))

The metal detector was applied along the wire fence line where the Niihau residents said the Zero punched through (see Position B, Primary Site Survey-GPS deleted). The ground near the fence and into the access road was saturated with modern metallic trash, ending hopes for a quick and thorough inspection for 60 year old evidence. Keith Robinson confirmed with the locals the direction that the aircraft came from as it approached the fence. Looking in the direction that they indicated there is a down slope of about 15 degrees. That means that the aircraft's final approach heading was about 40 degrees, and the ground was rising up to meet it.

An important feature of the original crash photos is that the section of wire fence so prominent in the background is not damaged. The aircraft's longitudinal axis is not perpendicular to the fence line but almost at a 45 degree angle to it. This implies that the aircraft yawed to the right after crashing through the fence and that the period photos taken at quartering angles did not show the damaged fence section. If it did not yaw then it had to have approached from the direction of the gate at Position C (GPS deleted) which discounts the Niihau resident's accounts.

Published accounts state that the aircraft's landing gear was sheared off when it hit the fence and the Niihau residents maintain this story today. It is difficult to imagine the lightly built nature of this fence shearing off the carrier duty designed landing gear of a two ton airplane approaching at 80 knots. A more likely scenario is that the aircraft struck the rising ground hard just at the fence and the subsequent boulders did the rest.

One factor that agrees with the Niihau resident's opinion of the aircraft's approach heading is the prevailing wind direction which is almost always from the north east. Any pilot executing an emergency landing on an unknown surface would want to have his ground speed as slow as possible and always land into the wind. The hypothetical approach from Position C would have him coming over a higher elevation ridge just before touching down with a strong cross wind.

Zero Post Crash Storage Site

Soon after the crash, military authorities came on island to inspect the wreckage. According to Keith Robinson, there was some concern that the Zero laying exposed in an open area might attract unwanted attention in case the Japanese returned. The Cletrac was used to tow the wreck down slope 100-150 yards about 200 degrees from Position B under the concealment of trees. The majority of the dismantling by U.S. personnel was done here.

Keith Robinson remembered playing in the wreckage here until he was about 12 years old. A photo credited to the Rev. H. Smith taken in 1942 shows an unidentified officer kneeling in front of the wreckage which has already been pulled apart and had skin stripped off. There are tree branches in close proximity in the background.

It was hoped that there would still be evidence of the disassembly work done here and some discarded parts might be found. Unfortunately, this entire area has now been turned into a garbage dump, and graded heavily with a bulldozer. One of the trees Keith remembered shading the wreck was dead and knocked over with indications of grading around it. Some exploration with the VLF detector was attempted but modern metallic trash, the physical nature of the site and time prevented any real examination. It was concluded that the only real hope of locating any further components that may have existed here would require a large scale excavation — obviously beyond the context of this visit.

Cletrac and Plow

The Cletrac and its plow had been used at least until the late 50s and then parked. Since its current location was in no way significant to any of its historically notable activities, this was primarily just a photographic inspection. The machine has advanced corrosion and is an obvious non-runner but is basically complete. It's small, bluff stature is an excellent sidebar to the Mitchell/Grant/Robinson Niihau furrow story. The Cletrac is parked near the warehouse where the Japanese pilot and his fellow conspirators locked up Hanaiki Niau in the attempt to control their deteriorating situation. GPS coordinates of the tractor's location were recorded and then later deleted per Robinson's request.

Dry lake furrow cross hatching

Due to the dry conditions, we were able to access one of the dry salt lakes on foot to examine evidence of the furrowing. From the helicopter's perspective on the in bound flight we were able to observe and photograph surviving furrow impressions in the south western quadrant of Halulu dry lake. From the ground the furrows are far less defined — their shape and track are more readable from the slightly different hue of soil that filled them in rather than any real topographical depression. The width of the furrows measures in between 2.5 and 3 feet and on the dry lake floor run arrow straight. At this site the most discernable were on a 200 degree/20 degree track with hints of an almost perfect 90 degree intersect at 90 to 100 foot increments. Keith Robinson reported that the headings were not constant over the whole island but were randomly applied as the terrain allowed. Most of the island is now heavily overgrown with "sour grass" and other vegetation which has obliterated furrows outside the salt pans.

PBY crash site

PAM's inspection party was driven to the beach immediately adjacent to a PBY crash site. The incident is somewhat historically controversial as the U.S. military investigators ruled the accident as an accidental stall contrary to Niihau eyewitnesses claiming that the PBY was shot down by a Japanese submarine that the PBY was attacking. There were several survivors from the PBY who were hospitalized.

Keith Robinson showed us the site to see if we had any interest in it. The huge waves continually breaking along this western shoreline would have long ago dispatched any traces of the PBY's shallow water impact site. Only the engines might still be present but in this environment they would have been heavily degraded as well. It was determined that the cost of bringing a survey boat over with a magnetometer to locate the engines was far beyond their historical value. PAM's onsite staff unanimously agreed that the effort was beyond their present interest.

APPENDIX 5

Korematsu v. United States

CIVIL LIBERTIES ACT OF 1988
Enacted by the United States Congress
August 10, 1988

"The Congress recognizes that, as described in the Commission on Wartime Relocation and Internment of Civilians, a grave injustice was done to both citizens and permanent residents of Japanese ancestry by the evacuation, relocation and internment of civilians during WWII.

As the Commission documents, these actions were carried out with out adequate security reasons and without any acts of espionage or sabotage documented by the Commission, and were motivated largely by racial prejudice, wartime hysteria, and a failure of political leadership.

The excluded individuals of Japanese ancestry suffered enormous damages, both material and intangible, and there were incalculable losses in education and job training, all of which resulted in significant human suffering for which appropriate compensation has not been made.

For these fundamental violations of the basic civil liberties and constitutional rights of these individuals of Japanese ancestry, the Congress apologizes on behalf of the Nation"

SOURCE: Street Law & The Supreme Court Historical Society presents:

Civil Liberties Act of 1988, Korematsu v. United States
http://www.streetlaw.org/en/landmark/cases/korematsu_v_united_states

APPENDIX 6

DIRECTOR

𝔉𝔢𝔡𝔢𝔯𝔞𝔩 𝔅𝔲𝔯𝔢𝔞𝔲 𝔬𝔣 𝔍𝔫𝔳𝔢𝔰𝔱𝔦𝔤𝔞𝔱𝔦𝔬𝔫
𝔘𝔫𝔦𝔱𝔢𝔡 𝔖𝔱𝔞𝔱𝔢𝔰 𝔇𝔢𝔭𝔞𝔯𝔱𝔪𝔢𝔫𝔱 𝔬𝔣 𝔍𝔲𝔰𝔱𝔦𝔠𝔢
𝔚𝔞𝔰𝔥𝔦𝔫𝔤𝔱𝔬𝔫, 𝔇. 𝔠.

PERSONAL AND ~~CONFIDENTIAL~~
BY SPECIAL MESSENGER

Major General Edwin M. Watson
Secretary to the President
The White House
Washington, D. C.

Dear General Watson:

          I thought the President and you might be interested
in the incident of a Japanese pilot being forced down in
his plane on December 7, 1941, on the outlying Island of
Niihau, Territory of Hawaii, where, with the aid of two Japanese, one a citizen and one an alien, he gained possession
of firearms and terrorized the natives, who were ignorant
of the existence of war, until overcome and killed on December
13, 1941, by a Hawaiian native he had shot and wounded. A
memorandum covering the details of this incident is transmitted herewith.

          With assurances of my highest regards,

                              Sincerely,

                              J. E. Hoover

Enclosure

The date on the document would appear to be Mar. 23 1942

Mn 2.1 102

M E M O R A N D U M

On Sunday, December 7, 1941, between 1:00 p.m. and 2:00 p.m., the natives of the outlying Island of Niihau, Territory of Hawaii, observed two airplanes flying low over the island. One flew on west past the island and was not seen again. The other, apparently out of gasoline, crashed near the home of Howard Kaleohano, a native Hawaiian on the outskirts of Nonopapa Village. Kaleohano rushed to the plane, which to his surprise he noted was not American, and, observing the Japanese pilot therein, pistol in hand, trying to disengage himself from his safety belt, wrenched the pistol from him and pulled the pilot out of the plane. Kaleohano also searched the pilot and his plane, securing all papers, which included a map of Oahu, the main Hawaiian Island on which the city of Honolulu, the Pearl Harbor Naval Base, and other important military installations are located.

By that time the native Hawaiian population from Nonopapa Village arrived on the scene and the pilot surrendered. The pilot, whose name was never ascertained, appeared friendly and peaceful and therefore at first was not held in custody, but was allowed to roam free, being fed and sheltered in the home of one of the natives. At first, when spoken to, he would reply in English writing, but later he spoke fluent English to the native populace. Possibly he was educated on the American Mainland.

It should be noted that the residents of the Island of Niihau, at that time, did not know of the existence of a state of war between the United States and Japan, nor of the Japanese raids on the Pearl Harbor Naval Base. The Island of Niihau has no communication with the other islands of the Hawaiian group, except by boat, and no boat stopped at that island from the outbreak of hostilities until Sunday morning, December 14, 1941. During the intervening period, however, on Monday and Tuesday, December 8 and 9, 1941, the natives took the aviator to Keei, where a sampan from the Island of Kauai was expected to call, in order to send him back to the proper authorities. The sampan didn't show up, and they could not launch a whaleboat stationed there because the sea was too rough. Also, on the night of Friday, December 12, 1941, the natives attempted, from the top of Paniau, the highest mountain on Niihau, to signal the Island of Kauai, by means of kerosene lamps and reflectors, but it does not appear that these messages got through to Kauai.

On Wednesday, December 10, 1941, the pilot was placed under loose guard at the home of Yoshio Harada, a Japanese of American citizenship. On Thursday, Harada sent a message to Ishimatsu Shintani, a Japanese alien resident on Niihau, to come to see him. These were the only two Japanese on the island. On Friday morning, December 12, 1941, Shintani went to Harada's house and there conferred with the Japanese pilot and Harada. The Hawaiians on guard at the Harada house do not know what they talked about, as they conversed in the Japanese language.

On Friday, December 12, 1941, Shintani went to the house of Kaleohano
and attempted to obtain from him the papers Kaleohano had taken from the
pilot and out of his plane. Shintani stated it was a "life and death matter",
and indicated he desired to destroy the papers by burning. Kaleohano showed
the papers to Shintani, but refused to give them to him, even though Shintani
offered a money bribe of about $200.00.

Sometime during Friday afternoon, the Japanese pilot, under
guard at Harada's house, by Harada and a Hawaiian native, cooperated with
Harada to overpower the Hawaiian guard and secure Harada's shotgun. The
aviator and Harada locked the guard in one of Harada's warehouses. They
then stopped a native Hawaiian woman on the nearby road, ordered her and her
children, at the point of the shotgun, to dismount from her horse-drawn
wagon, commandeered it, and drove off in the direction of the plane crash.

At the scene of the plane crash, they found a sixteen year old boy
guarding the plane. Kaleohano observed the aviator, Harada, and the boy
approaching his house at about 5:30 p.m., Harada prodding the boy in the
back with his shotgun. Kaleohano hid from them in his outhouse. They entered
Kaleohano's home, searched it, and apparently recovered the Japanese pilot's
pistol which Kaleohano had taken from him at the time of the crash. When
they left and went back to the plane, Kaleohano came out of hiding and
changed the papers to another hiding place away from his house. Kaleohano
then gave the alarm to Nonopapa Village that the men were on the rampage and
most of the native populace fled to the mountains or the forest.

About dusk Friday, the aviator and Harada captured two native
Hawaiians and forced them to help dismount the two machine guns from the
plane, loading them and a large pile of cartridges onto the wagon which they
had commandeered. The captives heard and observed the Japanese pilot get
into the plane, turn on the radio, put on the earphones, and make calls,
talking in Japanese. However, they did not hear him receive any reply.

One of these Hawaiians escaped from the aviator and Harada, and
went to the beach where he enlisted the aid of Benny Nokaka Kanahele in
attempting to secure the cartridges which had been removed from the plane,
inasmuch as Harada had told him that there were enough cartridges there to
kill every man, woman, and child on the island. He and Kanahele went to the
wagon and found it deserted and unguarded. Harada and the aviator had gone
off seeking to find more natives, and apparently took the machine guns with
them, as they were not on the wagon. Kanahele and the other Hawaiian took
the cartridges and hid them on the beach.

During Friday night and early Saturday morning, the aviator and
Harada burned the plane and Kaleohano's house, evidently hoping to destroy
the aviator's papers in the conflagration. They also went through Nonopapa
Village shooting off their guns and otherwise terrorizing the natives, most
of whom had fled into the forest and to the mountains. No natives were

- 3 -

killed, but they captured several, including Benny Kanahele and his wife.

On Saturday, December 13, 1941, at about 10:00 a.m., Kanahele attempted to snatch the pistol from his captor, the pilot, but failed. Kanahele's wife, who was next to him, then grabbed for the pistol and Harada snatched her away. The pilot, who still retained his pistol, shot Kanahele three times, inflicting flesh wounds in the right and left thighs and on his upper right side. Kanahele then picked up the pilot bodily and dashed his head against a stone wall killing him. Harada thereupon turned his gun on himself, shot himself twice in the abdomen, and died soon afterward.

Early Saturday morning, December 13, 1941, at 12:30 a.m., six strong Hawaiians, including Kaleohano, launched the whaleboat at Keei and after a trip of about 15 hours, rowed to the Island of Kauai, Territory of Hawaii, where they reported to Elmer Robinson, an American resident, who reported to the American Naval authorities, the facts as to the presence of the Japanese pilot on the Island of Niihau, and how, with the aid of the two Japanese on the island, they had terrorized and intimidated the native populace. A squad of twelve soldiers left Kauai late Saturday afternoon, aboard a lighthouse tender, arriving at the Island of Niihau on Sunday morning, December 14, 1941, where they found that the pilot and Harada had already been disposed of. Shintani, the alien Japanese who had tried to bribe Kaleohano, and Mrs. Ymeno Harada, the wife of the Japanese citizen, were arrested and are now incarcerated at Wailua Jail, on the Island of Kauai, in the custody of the military authorities. Benny Kanahele and his wife were also brought back to Kauai and given medical treatment.

APPENDIX 7

Life on Niihau in the 1940s: The Moroz photo collection

Photographs taken on Niihau during the 1940s are extremely rare, particularly those portraying everyday life on the island. In 1948, a young sailor named Eugene Moroz was posted to the Coast Guard's LORAN (LOng RAnge Navigation) station erected at Leahi on Niihau.

Eugene used his photography hobby to help pass the time, and in doing so captured many unique images of the people, activities and even extremely camera shy Aylmer Robinson on the island. Since Niihau had changed so little since before World War II, they give wonderful insights into life on the island as it would have been leading up to Nishikaichi's landing. The author extends many thanks to Mr. Moroz for allowing these photos to be published here for the first time.

The entrance gates to the Robinson family house area at Kiekie, Niihau. The road to the left goes to Nonopapa, the road at right is the inland route that guard Hanaike Niheu took after he escaped from the honey warehouse.

Niihau whale boat in its storage shed at Kii Landing. This is where the whale boat was launched from when Howell Kaleohano and the others made their dangerous night time passage to Kauai to alert the authorities about the Nishikaichi/Harada situation.

Niihau islanders launching the whale boat into the surf from Kii Landing. The eastern Niihau cliffs and Pueo Point are in the background - the photo was taken facing almost due south. The sea conditions between Niihau and Kauaiare were usually quite rough, making a night crossing particularly dangerous.

Above: A small stone pier at Kii Landing that existed through WWII. Pueo Point is in the far right background. Niihau men are carrying sheep to be loaded into the whale boat which is tied to its usual working place along side the pier. This pier was eventually destroyed by high surf.

Right: Crewman Yuzuru Okuhara sits on wooden boxes filled with pigeons aboard the "Lehua." He would eventually become a boat captain on the Niihau run. He was also a carpenter and later became a Christian minister. Okuhara built the casket for Lester Robinson, Keith and Bruce Robinson's father.

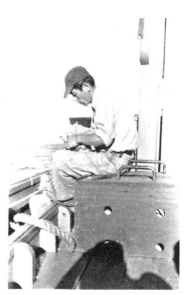

Left: An unidentified Niihau ranch foreman or truck driver writing notes at the Kii landing.

Below: Draft horses dragging a load of off-loaded lumber up the same dune. A cattle chute fence for loading livestock is visible in the background. Draft horses like these were initially used for pulling the plow to furrow the island after Major Brant's meeting with Aylmer, until the arrival of the Cletrac tractor.

Right: Aylmer Robinson talking with an unidentified military officer at Kaununui Landing in the hot glare of sun and sand.

Below: Aylmer Robinson supervising work on Niihau from horseback. Both Aylmer and his brother Lester hated to be photographed, but somehow Eugene Moroz managed to capture natural images of Aylmer going about his work.

Above: Dr. Kuhns aboard the "Lehua" heading for Niihau. Doctors who visited Nii-hau to check on the health of the islanders were family friends who also performed services for the Robinson family. Dr. Kuhns delivered Keith Robinson in 1941. To-day, islanders visit doctors on Kauai via the Robinson helicopter.

Below: The Niihau people at Kaununui Landing with Aylmer Robinson.

Above: Aylmer Robinson reads a letter in the pilot house of the "Lehua." He never used reading glasses, even in his later years.

Left: The Coast Guard LORAN antenna with the Quonset hut where Eugene Moroz was stationed.

Above: Lehua Island seen from the southeast. This extinct volcano cone is just off the north shore of Niihau. The PBY that crashed off Niihau on December 16, 1941 went down on the right and just out of frame of this picture on the northwest coast of Niihau.

Below: Just after sunrise, a crewman (either Yuzuru Okuhara or Haruo Kimura) works the trolling lines off the stern of the "Lehua" as it departs Kauai for Niihau. The black smoke in the background is from burning sugar cane on the Robinson plantation. Burning the cane fields is part of the harvesting process.

"Lehua" being loaded with honey cans and cases at Kaununui Landing for the trip back to Kauai. Ishimatsu Shintani, the reluctant participant in the Nishikaichi/Harada event, was largely responsible for the success of honey production. The "Lehua" had its own small boat carried on her starboard side alongside the pilot house.

INDEX

191

195

About the Author

Syd Jones has worked for several aviation museums as a restoration specialist including the Pacific Aviation Museum-Pearl Harbor as the founding Restoration Director and later as Interim Curator. He has had a lifetime interest in actively pursuing lost history, previously working for almost two decades on maritime archaeological recovery expeditions, including the richest Spanish galleon ever recovered, the Nuestra Senora De Atocha. The inside story of this highly publicized event was captured by Syd in his previous book "Atocha Treasure Adventures: Sweat of the Sun, Tears of the Moon".

Syd and his wife KT have visited many WWII European and Pacific battlefields, and have flown for years on the airshow circuit in WWII military aircraft, including the Centennial of Flight commemoration and Doolittle Raiders reunions.

When not attending to their avian family, Syd and KT can often be found flying their own WWII T-6 advanced combat trainer en route to their next adventure.

Made in the USA
Monee, IL
04 November 2023

45653503R00118